THE ROMANCE OF BETHNAL GREEN

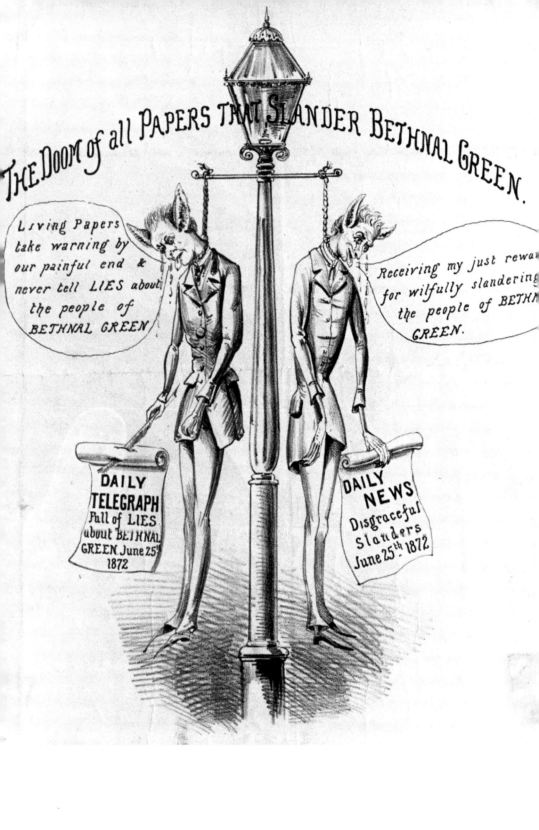

THE ROMANCE
OF BETHNAL GREEN

A TALE OF LONDON, PAST AND PRESENT

Cathy Ross

BACTON BOOKS
2007

First published in Great Britain in 2007
by Museum of London Archaeology Service
for Bacton Books, PO Box 60410, London E2 0WA

Designed by Tracy Wellman
Printed by Aldgate Press Ltd

ISBN 978 1 901992 74 8

Dr Cathy Ross is Head of the Department of Later London History at the Museum of London

Peter Marshall is a photographer and writer whose images of London since the 1970s can be seen on www.mylondondiary.co.uk

Paddy Killer is a textile artist whose work can be seen on www.paddykillerart.co.uk

CONTENTS

ILLUSTRATIONS

* courtesy Tower Hamlets Local History Library
** © Paddy Killer
All photographs by Peter Marshall © Peter Marshall
All uncredited photographs © the author

Bethnal Green c. 1930 (– • – • – = borough boundary)

INTRODUCTION

'Hardly a mile north-east of "the" City, tucked away behind the North Eastern Railway, is a little corner of London known as Bethnal Green. Comparatively few people know it except when they rush through the railway junction bearing its name when they get a vision of a sea of roofs crowded together and enveloped by a pall of smoke. But it has a population of 108,000 and is palpitating with life and activity.'

Percy A. Harris, 1934.

This is a book about the place where I live. London became my home 12 years ago, when I arrived for a job. Coming from the north of England, I did of course hold strong personal convictions about the capital. But the job was far too good to turn down and so I ended up in the city that I had so often, and so loudly, professed to dislike.

Once here, it was a different story. Pride and prejudice dissolved into thin air within a matter of days as London delivered its *coup de foudre*. Reader, I married it. And so, in 1993, there I was. Staring at the view from my tower block flat in East London, hopelessly smitten, my heart irrevocably pledged to the extraordinary city spread out so magnificently on the ground before me. My view stretches for miles. It makes you think you are looking right across the whole of London to its far edges. Westwards, the view is cut short by the lop-sided, high-rise skyline of the City. But to the south your eye flies over the Canary Wharf tower, past the green curves of Greenwich and Crystal Palace and on into the distance to the misty grey hills of Kent beyond. The exhilaration of this view has never failed to move me with feelings of awe and wonder. Trains, planes and automobiles move through it. Sunsets and dawns come and go. Buildings rise and fall. But the sheer magnificence of the city always produces an echo of that urban epiphany familiar to everyone who falls in love with London. It is the feeling that overcame Charles Lamb as he walked the crowded streets in the early nineteenth century, 'shedding tears in the motley Strand from fullness of joy at so much Life'.

The westward view is the most dramatic and divides itself into two layers. At the top stand the vertical shapes of the City towers; at the bottom lie the horizontal

Left: 'The Blind Beggar of Bethnal Green' by Elizabeth Frink (1957), Cranbrook Estate 2005.

planes of the low-rise roofs of Bethnal Green, which is where my tower block stands. Bethnal Green is traditionally 'the heart' of the East End, the old homeland for London's working-class masses. But Bethnal Green is a heart at the edge of the body. To the west, Bethnal Green shares a border with the City, the homeland to London's merchant kings. Part of Bethnal Green's distinctive character has always been its location, both near and far to the fabulous wealth that drives the capital. From my window the difference between the two is clearly visible. The high-rise landscape in the distance glitters in the daylight, shines at night and seems at the same time both fixed and dynamic, the buildings constantly erupting like volcanic plugs, re-shaping constantly, forcing themselves into new shapes as new fissures crack open and new formations push up to the surface. This is all in contrast to the dark and static flatness in the foreground. Bethnal Green seems to be still brooding on its Victorian reputation as a stagnant pond, a place where change is slower and less welcome.

The view from ground level was of course very different. I initially found East London both strange and familiar. Parts reminded me of Gateshead, particularly the thriving home bakery on Roman Road with its warm smells and permanent queue of old locals; loud, loquacious and very much at home. The occasional noisy seagull, combined with a 1950s café still advertising the fame of its prize-winning home-made ice-cream, had a faint echo of Morecambe's seaside melancholy. There was a good butcher; fruit and veg. came on market stalls and the streets seemed full of pensioners. Unlike the North, my middle-class accent blended easily in to the local soundscape but I was at first rather taken aback to be greeted in shops as 'madam', rather than 'love' or 'pet'. Was this a touch of deference or a hint of rudeness? I couldn't decide and eventually put the madam habit down to custom and practice.

There were noticeable differences between London and the North. The people, including the pensioners, were more racially diverse. The street litter was more abundant, as were the signs, notices and graffiti attached to every available surface. Everyone in Bethnal Green, it seemed, had decided to make his or her views known. In public. In writing. The divide between public and private behaviour had evidently long since broken down, but lying down on the pavement in the middle of the day somehow seemed a less bizarre a thing to do in the East End of London than it would be in the West End of Newcastle. People talked a lot. Shouting in the streets was the rule. And singing in the streets was positively encouraged, particularly for market stallholders.

Most exciting of all, Bethnal Green was a kind of living history wonderland, where bits of the past survived alive and well, albeit old and battered. Red Routemaster buses rolled through the streets. A John Soane church crumbled away on the corner. Nearby, you could open an iron gate and enter a miraculously charming

Victorian public garden complete with enamel signs, delicately edged with rust. Bethnal Green boasted a complete typography of social housing through the ages, and a fine display of shop fronts from all decades of the twentieth century. There were eel pie and mash shops from the 1950s, sweet shops with interiors from the 1920s and iron-wheeled market trolleys that reeked of Dickens. When I first came across the description of Bethnal Green as 'life-encrusted ground' I thought it suited the place, with its layers of the past all fused into a thick, colourful and grimy patina of past and present.

And yet the life-encrusted layers never seemed to set solidly. As I got to know the district better I realised that Bethnal Green was constantly fidgeting. Nothing ever stood still for long. The encrustations were constantly jostling for space and the comings and goings gave the place a kind of shanty-town feel as if everything was in transit and nothing was expected to last long term. Even the small shops on the Bethnal Green Road seemed to be temporary squatters, no more fixed than the market trolleys that were wheeled out across the pavements daily. Property occupation seemed to be more about chancing your luck, rather than making a serious commitment. At that time the building societies had not arrived in Bethnal Green Road, and there were no chain stores with the two important exceptions of Woolworths and Tesco. Bethnal Green was infused with a floating world quality alongside its life-encrusted materiality. Things changed as much as they stayed the same.

This socially-crunchy, life-encrusted fidgeting, with its strange mixture of age and transience, was a new urban mood for me and at first I wondered whether the distinctive sense of place I was experiencing was London in general rather than Bethnal Green in particular. But I soon came to realise that appreciating the difference between the various areas of London was a central part of being a Londoner, as was disagreeing about which area was the best. I, of course, became a born-again Bethnal Greener. I also came to be curious about the district's past.

Whether exceptional or typical, Bethnal Green was similar to all London's East End districts in that its past has already been well-mined by academics. There was no shortage of material with which to satisfy my curiosity. Not only was a wealth of primary research material to hand, but London's libraries offered a weighty freight of books, articles, analyses, and studies about East London: how the area has changed, what or who drove the changes, what did the changes mean for the capital and the nation. In this rich historiography, Bethnal Green plays a not insignificant part. It is rare to pick up a book on London's nineteenth-century poverty, or London's twentieth-century working class, and not to find Bethnal Green in the index. When it came to primary texts, Bethnal Green sometimes formed the whole substance of books, as for example in some of the best known sociological treatises of the 1950s: *Family and Kinship in East London* by Michael Young and Peter Willmott being the archetype.

This embarrassment of intellectual riches at first gave me a warm glow of pleasure at my good fortune in coming to live in such an interesting place. But over time, and perhaps inevitably, the warm glow of pleasure turned into a tiny flame of discontent. As (by now) a true Londoner and ruthless champion of the charms of my home district, I came to feel that Bethnal Green was somehow even more interesting and even more important than the existing historical narratives allowed. Although the territory of the East End's past had been well staked out, Bethnal Green's history contained episodes and events which, although known, remained puzzling, at least to my mind. The national museum that stood in the district intrigued me: as did the local history of silk weaving; and the district's extraordinary typography of tower blocks, in one of which I lived. I became a bit impatient. Why had these things happened here?

Alas, as a historian I had started to commit the sin of wearing my auto-ethnographic sub-text on my sleeve but all in all I came to believe two things. The first is that Bethnal Green has played a role different in kind to that played by other East End districts in the whole process of change and accommodation of otherness which has ebbed and flowed over London, shaping much of the city's life over the past 200 years. Bethnal Green, although unquestionably part of the East End, has had a different and distinctive past to the pasts of Stepney, Poplar, Stratford or Hackney. My second theory is that Bethnal Green's role has not only been distinctive but also critical. It is not just any old poor district, it has enjoyed a privileged position in the 'them' and 'us' relationship. Its life as 'the other' has played out in a way that has made it semi-us and semi-them, near and far at the same time. And because of its unique, chameleon-like qualities of insider / outsiderness, the effects of events in Bethnal Green have rippled out far beyond the borough's boundaries and into the life of the nation at large.

These two impulses are what lie behind this book. This is not a big picture account of urban change in the East End. Nor is it a local history of Bethnal Green. It is an episodic attempt to explore some of the ideas central to the former with reference to the things that happened on the ground in the latter. It is in part about the frames of mind that have shaped people's understanding of London over the past 150 years. It is certainly about interventions. Like all East End stories it is essentially about the encounter between separate parts of English society, divided from each other by variously defined differences: status, wealth, class and citizenship being the principal ones for the nineteenth and twentieth-century episodes described here.

Is there a meta-narrative that links these episodes of encounter? Yes (and here my personal feelings are very visible). The metaphor that seems to me to embrace some of the qualities of the cross-class relationship that played out in Bethnal Green, is a romance. In this narrative, the drivers of change in Bethnal Green are sentiment, fascination, curiosity, obsession and enchantment alongside the fear, rational deduction, moral duty or Christian mission that are more usually identified as the dynamic forces in the story of social improvement in London. A romance is not altogether a fanciful device. It has the attraction of allowing the cross-class encounter to be more of a human comedy than a mechanistic experiment in cause and effect. More often than not, the catalyst of change in Bethnal Green was unforeseen consequences and one could characterise the long process of interplay between the macro-world of middle-class ideas and the micro-world of Bethnal Green as one long comedy of errors. In all three of the encounters which form the heart of this book, chaos and misrule are players. Ideas usually end up translated into bricks and mortar at the opposite end of the ideological spectrum from the point at which they started.

A romantic analogy also allows some sense of the desire for psychological completeness to drive the action. In this analysis each party sees in the other the attraction of the very thing it lacks. The comfortably-off need the drama of struggle and Christian suffering; the poor need the reflected glamour of royalty and property. There was a cross-fertilisation at every level. As one of the Oxbridge undergraduate settlers who came to nineteenth-century Bethnal Green to do good put it, 'Oxford influences Bethnal Green and Bethnal Green reacts on Oxford'. A romance also allows some possibility of parity between the two protagonists. Nobody could deny that in terms of wealth and status Bethnal Green was the poor relation in the us and them story. But, as in the best romances, the party with the worldly wealth and choices does not necessarily hold the power in the relationship. The ability of the poorer party to triumph over adversity and reach fulfilment above and beyond social divisions is often what drives the plot forward.

It might also be mentioned that the romantic analogy suits Bethnal Green well given the place's famous ability to seduce its observers. Michael Young's objectivity as a sociologist was often called into question because of his undisguised admiration for his 'beloved' Bethnal Green. Stewart Headlam, the radical Anglo Catholic curate of St Matthew's church in the 1870s, called Bethnal Green an earthly paradise and declared that he loved it only less fondly than Eton. A recent study of the Victorian social settlements which brought Keble College theology students and Cheltenham Ladies College alumni to Bethnal Green in the 1880s have read a strong erotic charge into these encounters between rich and poor. The thrill persisted in the less febrile atmosphere of the twentieth-century settlements. 'We'd never met anything like the Bethnal Greeners. I mean it was another world altogether. ... Here am I coming from these exalted circles with all this blue blood coursing through my veins, and here are these slum children with naked feet and all the poverty which we'd all read about – (we were about fifty years out of date, but never mind, that was the picture we'd got into our heads) – and then when we did get there we found that Bethnal Green was at last educating us and God, how we needed it!' Even in the last decade of the twentieth century the place could still cast a spell on researchers: 'Bethnal Green is an exciting place to work – its sense of history, its contrasts and its people provide a special backdrop. Even the more mundane elements of the study have appeared stimulating in the Bethnal Green context.'

The chapters that follow explore the romance between Bethnal Green and the wider world by focussing on three episodes. The first chapter serves as a scene-setting introduction to the territory where the action happens. The second looks at the extraordinary episode from the 1870s whereby national government decided to erect and run at national expense a local museum in Bethnal Green. If the analogy of a romantic journey can be pushed to its limit, this represents the initial rebuff when wrong was done to poor old Bethnal Green by the ignorance and prejudice of its social superiors. The next chapter looks at the burden of ideological freight that was loaded on to the figure of the Bethnal Green silk weaver as the industry died a painful death in the nineteenth century only to be reborn again in the twentieth as the apotheosis of honest English craftsmanship. This could be said to represent the point when a spark of empathy between the two protagonists began to develop into a sentimental attachment. The fourth chapter sees sentiment grow into fascination and obsession. This essay looks at the 1950s, Bethnal Green's glamorous decade, when the borough became a hot-spot for sociologists, architects, town planners and intelligentsia of all complexions. It was in the 1950s that the insular, working-class district became transformed, Cinderella-like, into a model village of good community. Bethnal Green in the 1950s was suddenly discovered to be a shining New Jerusalem rather than the disorderly Babylon of its reputation.

The final chapter is where this narrative device runs into difficulties. This chapter leaps forward in time from London in the 1950s to London in 2005. Things in Bethnal Green, as all over the East End, ain't what they used to be. For one thing, Bethnal Green as an official patch of land is not so easy to define. In 1966 the territory formerly known as Bethnal Green was absorbed into the larger borough of Tower Hamlets. For another, the working class monoculture that shaped the us and them dynamic for so long is rapidly sinking down the life-encrusted layers, disappearing from view beneath a multicultural overlay. Where there was once effectively one 'them', there are now many 'thems'. The local government wards that correspond to the old borough have a new social topography with new loyalties. 36% of the population are from a Bengali background and the 53% from a white background are riddled with middle-class arrivals, such as myself, who have no family and kinship networks in the borough and can scarcely be said to fly the flag for the old Cockney essentialism, although we do live in the tower blocks.

Given the dramatic changes of recent times, the question inevitably arises: is the old romance dead? Have the old stories of us and them that drove social change in Bethnal Green until the second world war lost their potency as London moves on and other districts take their turn in the national spotlight. The 2005 general election in Bethnal Green, when the sitting Labour MP Oona King was dramatically ousted by the maverick and firey-tongued George Galloway provided much food for thought. There was the unmistakable whiff of old romance in the air as the missionary outsider parachuted in to help the helpless 'others' find their voice in a hard and cruel world. But was this a true romance or a false infatuation? This is all for the last chapter, and these are matters to which readers will undoubtedly bring their own thoughts.

The final point in this introduction is best made by returning to the view from my tower block. Looking at the past from the perspective of a resident does not, of course, give me any particular authority as a historian. Neither does it make my view of the past any more or less 'authentic' than someone writing about Bethnal Green from a tower block flat in Chicago. This is not any sort of insider story. However I do think that a local perspective shapes the sense you see in the past and the sensitivities you bring to bear on the material you look at. Seeing a place every day as it goes about its daily business almost certainly encourages you to take a long view, picking out the patterns that take shape over time. It also perhaps produces an organic view of the past in which everything is interconnected through the fact of local coincidence. In my case I am sure it has affected the way I see the 'us' and 'them' of London's past. There is no doubt that in Bethnal Green terms I am one of 'them', a middle-class incomer with a desk job beyond the boundaries and no family ties within. And yet every morning the view from my window places me here, physically distant from the 'them' over there. My hope at least is that this location has bred in me some empathy and respect for Bethnal Greeners of the past. In the pages that follow, their voices are faint compared to the many voices speaking for them or at them. But this is ultimately their story.

Overleaf: Crossland Square c. 1900.

1 PARISH TO BOROUGH

DIFFERENCE

'Each class in London has a neighbourhood or more properly a town of its own'
John Fisher Murray, *The World of London*, 1841.

All London's East End districts have been, at some point inthe past, one half in a tale of two cities: rich / poor; respectable / dangerous; middle class / working class; us / them. So what makes Bethnal Green's experience of being 'the other' distinctive? One thing that distinguishes it from its neighbours is the sheer quantity of traffic from rich to poor that came the district's way. From the 1840s onwards Bethnal Green attracted philanthropic and improving interventions in quantities quite disproportionate to its size. It was, as Ruth Glass observed in the 1940s, a heavily intervened-in place. 'In the middle of the nineteenth century, observers were still struck by the singular absence of public buildings. Churches, chapels, taverns and beer houses were the only meeting places. Some fifty years later Bethnal Green was noted for the very opposite: there was then, and there is now, an abundance of institutions; settlements, clubs, missions… In terms of its institutional equipment Bethnal Green is far richer than the more well to do parts of London and the newer suburbs and housing estates.'

This history of interventions is partly explained by the fact that Bethnal Green acquired otherness relatively early in the nineteenth century. By 1862, as noted by one account of London, it was thoroughly notorious as a 'dense, dingy, poverty-stricken suburb' in contrast to 'its more attractive and thriving neighbour Hackney'. As chapter three explores, Bethnal Green's otherness was directly connected to the life-cycle of the silk industry, the doomed trade which employed so many of the parish's families. Silk entered on its painful and prolonged death-throes almost from the start of the century. By the 1830s the parish's problems were well known and its catalogue of interventions underway. An example of an early Bethnal Green intervention is the scheme dreamt up by Bishop Blomfield, a utilitarian-minded Bishop of London who in 1836 proposed the formation of the Metropolitan New Churches Fund as a means to 'reclaim hundred and thousands of the poor from

Left: Victoria Park Cemetery entrance, 1986. Peter Marshall.

practical heathenism'. The assumption behind the scheme was simply that more churches would produce more church-goers. Bethnal Green, with only two Anglican churches for a population of 80,000, was the parish chosen to prove the point and accordingly ten new churches were erected between 1839 and 1849, leaving Bethnal Green as one of only two parishes in the country to boast a full set of churches dedicated to all twelve apostles. The Blomfield episode was a typical, indeed an archetypical, Bethnal Green intervention in that it failed spectacularly to create the expected improving effect. Blomfield's new churches remained empty and within ten years the bishop was shaking his head in sorrow over 'the spot where it is said that we sowed our seed in vain'. Fifty years later the episode was remembered only as an example of mindless philanthropy and wasted effort '...to such an extent that even now "Remember Bethnal Green" is apt to be thrown in the teeth of those who try to inaugurate any great movement in the city on behalf of the Church'.

Besides its full set of twelve apostle churches, Bethnal Green also boasted a complete set of British social housing types including examples from all the Victorian housing philanthropists. All phases of council housing were handsomely represented in the borough, including some much-acclaimed schemes, ranging from the London County Council's pioneering Boundary Street estate of the 1890s to Denys Lasdun's experimental 'cluster' tower blocks of the 1950s. Bethnal Green also contained the country's largest concentration of settlements, those residential communities established by schools and universities in the late nineteenth century to promote social intercourse between rich and poor. Toynbee Hall in Whitechapel is the best known example of a university settlement in the East End, but Oxford House in Bethnal Green opened in April 1884, predating Toynbee Hall by a few months. Of the fifty or so settlements still active in Britain by the 1940s five were within the borough's boundaries. These five brought some distinguished connections to Bethnal Green. Oxford House was Bethnal Green's link to Keble College Oxford; St Hilda's East, was established in 1889 by former pupils of Cheltenham Ladies College; St Margaret's House was the 'ladies branch of Oxford House' founded in 1893 and University House was another breakaway from Oxford House, with strong connections to Repton School in Derbyshire. Ridley House was a smaller university settlement founded in 1906. By the eve of the first world war Bethnal Green's borders also contained sixteen established churches, eleven dissenting churches, including one Catholic church for a Lithuanian sect, plus ten miscellaneous places of worship including chapels in schools or hospitals. There were ten missions, four synagogues, one Salvation Army citadel and one meeting house for the Society of Friends.

In addition to its school, college and Church connections, nineteenth-century Bethnal Green also found itself the focus of attention from both Crown and state. The Bethnal Green branch of the South Kensington museum opened in 1872, the only example in the country of a local museum maintained at national expense and a large exception to the rule that national government had no business with local affairs. Following the pattern set by the Blomfield churches, the promised social effects failed to materialise, leaving the museum as an embarrassing white elephant (as explored in chapter three). The Crown's interest was its purchase of a large parcel of land in the early 1840s to create a new public park, designed to improve the health of the artisan population and encourage a more genteel population to take up residence. Victoria Park was the result. Straddling the boundaries of Bethnal Green, Hackney and Poplar, the park imitated Regent's Park in that the Crown leased land around the edge to speculative builders, hoping thus to encourage residential development. On the Bethnal Green side, around Approach Road, builders created a few streets of relatively grand four-storey middle-class terrace houses, looming above the two-storey artisan terraces. The fashionable West End residents never moved east, as hoped, but this small patch of Crown property did create somewhere for Bethnal Green's better-off inhabitants to live.

The park and the museum were two of Bethnal Green's nineteenth century *grands projets*. The third was Columbia Market, a lavish and fantastical building erected by Angela Burdett-Coutts in the 1860s at a cost of £200,000. She wanted to do practical good for Bethnal Green's costermongers who, she imagined, would renounce their disreputable habits of trading in the streets and embark on a more orderly life in an indoor market: 'be sober, be vigilant, be pitiful, be courteous' said the gothic inscriptions over the door. The market was a spectacular building: a vast Flemish guildhall, bristling with portentous gargoyles and even attracting the admiration of modernist Nikolaus Pevsner as 'one of the great follies of the Victorian age'. Like the Bishop's churches and the government's museum, the Baroness's market also failed to realise the wishful thinking that had created it. By the 1890s, when Charles Booth's investigators came to Bethnal Green, Columbia Market remained empty: 'the people cling to their old ways, and the costermongers prefer to ply freely in the open streets'. By the mid-twentieth century the building was complete derelict. Despite Pevsner's calls for it to be preserved the gothic extravaganza was demolished in 1960 by the London County Council.

What was it about Bethnal Green that proved irresistible to do-gooding outsiders? Why in 1889 did Cheltenham Ladies College choose Bethnal Green as the site for their charitable settlement? Was it the same attraction that sixty years later led Michael Young to choose Bethnal Green as the home for his new Institute of Community Studies? Critical mass may be part of the explanation. The Institute of Community Studies, for example, grew from an existing infrastructure of social research associated with University House. Location, real and symbolic, may also be a factor. Bethnal Green was both far and near, outcast but within reach of redemption. Although it was a desperately poor district, poverty had not transformed itself into savagery, as it was perceived to have done in other parts of London. 'Bethnal Green is certainly something different from a vast Seven Dials,' said the *Saturday Review* in 1872, noting that despite the district's sad and dismal appearance and 'monotonous meanness and dullness' it had a 'humble but thriving working class'. Parts of Bethnal Green had 'two-room parish' status, meaning it contained families who had not yet sunk into the abyss of the underclass and could in theory be pulled back up to safety.

In Charles Booth's monumental survey of London's life and labour at the turn of the nineteenth century Bethnal Green came out with mixed colours. It had one of London's worst patches of dark blue and black streets, in the notorious Old Nichol, the 'Jago', at the Shoreditch end of the parish, but overall its streets were coded in light blue and pink, signifying 'rough English poverty'. 'Throughout Bethnal Green,' reported Booth's observers, 'there is a large amount of old-established poverty living in two storied "light blue" streets, the men being carmen, labourers of all sorts, furniture makers and bootmakers in a small way; coupled with this there is a large area of dark blue and black in St Paul's and St Matthew's parishes representing the very rough vicious class.' Bethnal Green was portrayed as having a different character to Wapping and Shadwell, both more tied to the river and dock culture. It was certainly distinct from Spitalfields and Whitechapel where the tone was set by 'Jews and common lodging houses and shelters' and where, according to Booth's investigators, 'wastrel poverty' was found – as opposed to the 'sturdy poverty' found in Bethnal Green.

The nuances of Bethnal Green, as portrayed in the Booth survey, are well illustrated by a passage in the volumes looking at religious influences, one of many passages laced with anti-Semitism. Moving into the Old Nichol from Spitalfields the writer detected a change of moral character. 'Crossing the barrier formed by the Great Eastern railway, we pass into another world. We leave behind us the floating population of common lodging-houses and night shelters, the low women of the "furnished rooms" and the foul but thriving poverty of the Jews. We are no longer struck by the foreign appearance of the streets; we are conscious of a different moral atmosphere; things are in some ways better, but in other ways worse; the people are more independent, but rougher mannered; and their poverty is certainly greater.' Bethnal Green was thus not beyond the pale. The district was not visibly alien, unlike the 'ghetto' that Whitechapel was perceived to have recently become. The degree of Bethnal Green's wretchedness created an impression of passivity. Although criminal black spots existed, it was not on the whole portrayed as an overly threatening place. Smallness is often mentioned as a Bethnal Green quality. The houses were doll's houses, the people were short and stunted, they shared their lives with small creatures. Caged birds, rabbits and guinea pigs, pigeons, dogs and goats were all part of the Bethnal Green landscape. It was a district of cat's meat, bone scraps and offal where people ate greasy faggots and cow heels. The word most usually used to describe the Bethnal Greeners is 'unfortunate' and the quality most usually conjured up is pathos: 'it is notorious that an enormous proportion of the people are unhealthy, without vigour or physical strength, pallid and cachectic, stunted in their growth and of feeble organisation… the very police are aware of the feeble physical powers of a Bethnal Green mob.' This stereotype of feeble victim-hood was a legacy of the silk weavers but the nineteenth century saw it embrace the district as a whole, casting Bethnal Green as a place of pathos. There was little to be scared of in Bethnal Green and much to be sentimental about.

The perceived weakness and passivity of the people translated well into both the Christian mind-set and the scientific one. From the Christian point of view such a place was the perfect location to discharge Christian responsibilities on the part of the rich to the poor. From the scientific point of view the perceived homogeneity of its poverty-stricken population made it the ideal social laboratory where experiments or observations could be carried out in a relatively controlled way. Us and them easily translates into experimenter and experimented on, and there is no shortage of nineteenth-century texts about Bethnal Green which seek to explain its problems using a scientific vocabulary of observation and hypothesis. In Hector Gavin's 1848 book, *Sanitary Ramblings,* Bethnal Green is presented as a type specimen: it is 'a type of the condition of the metropolis and other large towns'. Gavin explored the parish in meticulously systematic detail, presenting his readers with a gruesome catalogue of the district's open sewers and rancid streets. But his investigation of the local was designed to uncover universal truths. 'I was actuated by the conviction that I should find in that parish all those leading elements which tend to deteriorate the health and prematurely to destroy no inconsiderable proportion of the population of large towns.' The 1950s saw Bethnal Green again presented as a type specimen. But this time its observers found elements to improve the condition of large towns.

With the benefit of hindsight, it is easy to reflect that that if there is a scientific thread to be detected in the story of local change in Bethnal Green throughout the last two centuries it is certainly not the law of smooth progress through scientific deduction. Chaos and complexity theory seems a better fit given that what often moved matters forward was unintended consequences. However, for most of Bethnal Green's life as a parish and metropolitan borough, it was saddled with an image of simplicity, insularity and homogeneity which easily translated into ideal social laboratory, urban type, or even national archetype. Bethnal Green performed sterling service as shorthand for the nation's poorer or working-class communities. 'The yard does not vary from Aberdeen to Plymouth, and the pint pot contains as much in Mayfair as in Bethnal Green,' said the BBC in 1928, mapping the compass points of the nation in an effort to lay down some common principles of pronounciation. Altogether Bethnal Green presented an irresistible combination of high challenge and low threat. Its location placed it within reach. It was a needy yet safe place in which to do good, its image flavoured with a distinctively aromatic combination of pathos and sentiment.

Overleaf: 'The Dogs of Alcibiades' (installed 1912), Victoria Park, 1994. Peter Marshall.

PLACE

'The Green of Bethnal Green is but the memory of the Tudor village it once was; its colours now are those of smoke, soot, brick-dust and filtered sunlight. On that packed, life-encrusted ground of East London, time has put down three layers of living stones. Oldest of all the streets of sweating walls and puddled pavements – past homes of Huguenot weavers, immigrant Jews and the poverty-stricken freebooters of the Dickens novels. Most recent of all, the squat white boxes of the pre-fabs, where the war-born children crawl and clamber at their games. Behind and between rise the dark shapes of the Victorian Trust Buildings – the earliest workers' flats.'

Ruth Glass and Maureen Frenkel, 1946.

Bethnal Green was officially defined as a distinct patch of London with the creation of the parish of Bethnal Green in 1746. Its identity as a place was reinforced around 1900 with the arrival of the Metropolitan Borough of Bethnal Green, the body that took over from the parish as the modern, secular vehicle for local government. In turn the borough was overtaken by events after the second world war as new demands placed on London's local government made small units inefficient. The metropolitan borough was abolished in 1966 and the territory formerly known as Bethnal Green was absorbed into the larger and more administratively cost-effective unit of the London Borough of Tower Hamlets. Today, although its borders have inevitably become more fluid without the definition provided by its own borough council, Bethnal Green is still roughly in the same place it has always been.

The parish created in 1746 took land from the older parish of Stepney as a response to the eastwards march of bricks, mortar and journeymen weavers from Spitalfields, London's eighteenth-century, industrial boom-town. Although in 1900 the metropolitan borough assumed for itself a village pedigree, thinking of itself as growing out organically from a centre-point, Bethnal Green's pattern of growth was urban spread from its western edge. It was always a small place. Before it became a parish, it was a church-less hamlet at a crossroads, one mile from the City. As a metropolitan borough it was the 5th smallest in London with 759 acres or just under one and a half square miles. As a parish its tiny land area was hopelessly overwhelmed by the scale of its population increase. The 15,000 people in the parish in 1746, rose to 74,000 in 1846 and 130,000 on the parish's translation into a borough in 1901. This was Bethnal Green at its most life-encrusted and overcrowded, with a density of 171 persons to the acre.

The creation of the borough marked the turning of the population tide: influx turned to exodus as both the new borough and the larger London County Council (LCC) started encouraging people to move out. During the 1920s, many Bethnal Greeners ended up in Becontree, the mammoth LCC cottage estate built on marshland near Dagenham. By the outbreak of war in 1939 the borough's population had been slimmed down to 94,000. German bombs cleared the nineteenth century housing stock, as did slum clearance programmes and the depopulation continued after the war with planners working towards a target figure of 46,000 for the borough. The Bethnal Green diaspora resumed and many families moved out to Essex particularly the new town of Harlow. By 1956 the population had fallen to 54,000, reaching its target figure of 46,000 ten years later just as the old metropolitan borough was absorbed into the new London Borough of Tower Hamlets. Today, the population is on the rise again and the five wards in Tower Hamlets which roughly correspond to the old Bethnal Green territory (although covering a slightly larger area) recorded a population of 59,347 in the 2001 census.

Bethnal Green's reputation for overcrowding was matched by its reputation for insularity. Culturally, socially, economically and geographically, Bethnal Green was usually characterised as an inward-looking place. It was certainly landlocked. At a distance from the river Thames, it was hemmed in on the west by Shoreditch, the north by Hackney and on the south and the east by Stepney and Poplar respectively. The lack of diversity seen by many nineteenth-century observers as characteristic of East End life was magnified in Bethnal Green. Outsiders saw it as a monotonous place, its landscape made up of uniform terraced streets of two-storey cottages, its mono-cultural working-class inhabitants engaged in dull, unsatisfying toil. It was insular in transport terms, earning it the name 'the by-passed borough' and Ruth Glass's aside in 1946 that 'there are few reasons for going through Bethnal Green in order to get to some place of general importance'. It was only in December 1946, when London Underground extended the Central Line to Bethnal Green, that public transport really penetrated the territory.

Bethnal Green's administrative history does have one quirk: an apparent confusion as to where exactly its centre was. On eighteenth-century maps the name Bethnal Green was usually assigned to the church-less hamlet at the crossroads beneath Cambridge Heath. In 1746 this hamlet had given its name to the new parish but the new parish church of St Matthew's was built half a mile to the west, on the fringes of Spitalfields. One hundred and fifty years later, the new metropolitan borough moved its administrative centre away from the parish church and back to the greener and pleasanter crossroads. By this time the crossroads had acquired a church, one sufficiently historic to convey the illusion of being an ancient village parish church, even though it was actually an 1828 'Waterloo church'. St John's was sited besides a patch of common land which looked to all intents and purposes like a village green. Only the absence of a graveyard gave a clue that the church had not been embedded there since time immemorial. The erection nearby of the new Town Hall in 1910, the Council's first public library in 1922, and its show-piece York Hall and Central Baths in 1929, seemed to confirm that here indeed was the centre of Bethnal Green.

The parish church had been left stranded at the Spitalfields end of the borough but the Bethnal Green name migrated back towards it in the late 1980s when the area around it became one of Tower Hamlets seven 'neighbourhoods', an experiment in decentralised local government. Under this system Bethnal Green Neighbourhood included the western end of Bethnal Green together with wards formerly in Stepney. The old Town Hall, library and York Hall found themselves in Globe Town Neighbourhood. Today you can still see a few Bethnal Green Neighbourhood litter bins in the streets, co-existing with more recent themed street furniture conveying the message that the district formerly known as Bethnal Green Neighbourhood became in the mid-1990s 'Banglatown'. Under the neighbourhood system, all seven districts had colour coded street furniture: Bethnal Green's colour was green. Globe Town's was black. Banglatown's new lamp posts are multicoloured.

This shuttling backwards and forwards of Bethnal Green's centre could be said to symbolise a choice of pedigrees for Bethnal Green: urban district or rural village. The metropolitan borough liked to think of itself as the direct descendent of a green and pleasant agricultural village spreading outwards from its centre. The official seal it chose in 1900 was a figurative and somewhat pastoral image showing characters from a seventeenth-century ballad, the blind beggar of Bethnal Green his daughter and dog. A similar choice of urban or rural genealogy existed for many of London's metropolitan boroughs, particularly those with far greater village credentials than Bethnal Green, such as Hackney. However the village strand was particularly strongly internalised in Bethnal Green's sense of itself.

PEOPLE

'No corner of London is more conscious of itself. The majority of the inhabitants are proud of belonging to it, resent having to leave it, and as often as not, take the earliest opportunity to return to it.'

Percy A. Harris, 1934.

Who were the Bethnal Greeners, the people who lived inside this landlocked metropolitan oblong which thought of itself as a village? Nineteenth-century observers generally painted a motley picture. Bethnal Green was a place of small tradesmen, the self-employed, the under-employed and the underclass. 'Its men,' according to John Hollingshead in 1861, 'are mainly poor dock labourers, poor costermongers, poorer silk-weavers clinging hopelessly to a withering handicraft, the lowest kind of thieves, the most ill-disguised class of swell-mobsmen with a sprinkling of box and toy makers, shoe-makers and cheap cabinet-makers. Its women are mainly hawkers, sempstresses, the coarsest order of prostitutes and aged stall-keepers, who often sit at the street corners in old sedan chairs.' Silk weaving was the most prominent local industry around 1800 to be supplanted by furniture-making and the boot and shoe trade by 1900. In all three cases, small workshops, self-employment and domestic industry was the norm and even by the 1940s the district included only a dozen firms employing over 100 people. In addition to the staple trades of clothing and furniture-making 'which,' according to the Booth survey, 'give a stamp of peculiarity to the streets of Bethnal Green', there were 'large numbers of costermongers living and pursuing their loud vocation here, and there are also many small shopkeepers and others who live on supplying the wants of the poor; while at the bottom the population passes through the doubtful paths of the "fancy" into those of the professional thief.' Men, women and children lived with animals and birds, which they enthusiastically bought, sold, bred, compared, kept, raced, betted on and ate. By the 1920s Bethnal Green was the rabbit-breeding and song-bird-dealing capital of London.

The district's economy was thus a thing of shreds and patches which left its inhabitants peculiarly vulnerable to the forces of modernity. As factory production came to dominate most branches of manufacturing so the individual effort of workshop or home-based artisans lost value. Most notoriously, the hand-loom silk weaving industry that had created the parish in the eighteenth century collapsed in the nineteenth, transforming a body of hard working artisans into a wretched mass of human flotsam. The potential for socially useful workers to 'sink' in life and be reconfigured, Frankenstein-like, as the socially dangerous underclass was one of Bethnal Green's dark dynamics. The typical, indeed stereotypical, picture of the nineteenth-century Bethnal Greener was of a person teetering on the edge of the poverty abyss, if not already falling into it.

Within this overall picture of hand to mouth existence there were two relatively common stereotypes. The first was the 'wretched creature', those poor unfortunates who had fallen so far from the norms of human existence that they had been virtually reduced to the state of the animals they lived with. This type was particularly well represented by the hand-loom weavers, more sinned against than sinning and generating compassion rather than disapproval. They were often presented as 'deserving', in the terms of the day, in that their wretchedness was combined with 'heroic endurance under the most frightful trials… and they make us respect these poor creatures even in their dirt and rags'. This was John Hollingshead in 1861, describing weaver families living in the Old Nichol. The children were 'ragged, sharp weasel like', the adults were sickly and 'sinking with anxiety, if not from want'.

The second stereotype was the 'cheerful rough': 'hard working people, who work honestly for their living and get drunk on Saturday night'. These were identified by their loud behaviour and their fondness for drink. 'There is much life and good humour in the streets, noted Booth's investigators. 'Heavy drinking is said to be a sure sign that work is plentiful… the police are busiest when the people are most prosperous – or would be so if it was not for the drink.' Another characteristic was their general failure to behave with due decorum: 'weddings we are told are the occasion of a drunken orgy, the disorder extending even to the church'. These Bethnal Greeners were seen less as victims but as people with choices which they chose to exercise badly. Discipline and strength were more appropriate responses than compassion and understanding.

These two stereotypes made their way into the twentieth century. By the 1920s Bethnal Greeners were less often likened to animals but their wretchedness had turned into passivity. The two most commonly heard phrases, noted Constance Harris in 1926, were 'mustn't grumble' and 'Gawd is good'. She saw a 'lack of sustained effort and concentration' and 'an acceptance of things as they are' in most of the things she observed. Roughness was still much in evidence: young women drinking was 'a common sight and is thought to be no degradation'. She saw men and women sitting at their windows watching the life of the streets 'doing absolutely nothing but smoke or eat fruit, dropping the skins on the heads of the passers by'. By the 1930s roughness could be seen as not altogether bad. 'The Bethnal Greener is a type, and a good type too. Sturdy, independent, perhaps a bit rough but a good friend, and once he knows you, extraordinarily loyal'. By the 1940s they were being allowed a little more complexity. P.J.O. Self viewed the Bethnal Green character as a mixture of things: 'they have been described as hard-boiled and apathetic, and also as warm-hearted, responsive and friendly. Both descriptions can be right, because they refer to two different spheres of behaviour. The latter attitude is the one seen in their social and day to day life and in helping each other in adversity. The former is the attitude taken to education, to Culture and to the established order of Church and State.'

But what did the Bethnal Greeners have to say for themselves? Somewhat predictably, the reported speech of nineteenth-century Bethnal Greeners reveals a remarkable ability to mirror what the interviewer wants to hear. On the opening of the Bethnal Green Museum in 1872 some journalists portrayed the Bethnal Greeners as possessing a natural talent for art appreciation. A *Daily Telegraph* reporter claimed that 'the crowd who peered intently on the works of Meissonier might have been a crowd of connoisseurs.' Elsewhere it was recounted that a 'well known artist' was impressed with the 'candid exclamations and rough judgment' of the people. 'I heard him say to a friend that he was never so struck in his life at the unerring taste of the poor people's criticism'. Although the credit for this remarkable fact was often given to the exhibits rather than the people ('everybody entitled to give evidence on the subject thoroughly knows that the commanding influences of the best art make itself immediately felt by the vulgar'), the idea was sufficiently seductive to take root, although Henry James made his scepticism very clear. Going to the museum on a paying day he saw no locals 'so we are obliged to repeat from hearsay a graceful legend that the masses, when admitted, exhibit as one man, a discrimination of which Mr Ruskin himself might be proud, and observe and admire on the very soundest of principles.'

By the twentieth century Bethnal Greeners were considered better able to speak for themselves, although the kindly prompt of the social researcher can often be detected in the background. Whatever the difficulties in disentangling the 'authentic' Bethnal Green voice, one opinion seems remarkably consistent over both centuries, the fact that Bethnal Greeners liked living in Bethnal Green. Booth's investigators reported in the 1890s that despite the district's privations and hardships, they found 'respectable poor folk who are proud of their gardens … and avowing that "it would be impossible to find a nicer house or a better copper or a pleasanter place to live in".' By the 1950s such views were recorded with approval rather than surprise. 'I suppose people who come here from outside think it's an awful place, but us established ones like it,' said one Bethnal Green mother to Michael Young and Peter Willmott. Another declared: 'I was born and bred in Bethnal Green and my parents and their parents before them: no, I wouldn't leave Bethnal Green, I wouldn't take a three-penny bus ride outside Bethnal Green.' By the 1960s even adolescent boys felt mellow towards the place: 'I like Bethnal Green – its my home town. I know the place and I know the people. I'd like to go on living here.' The same study, it should be noted, recorded the odd dissenter 'I want to get as far away as possible from Bethnal Green. There's no social life in Bethnal Green, no appreciation of the arts – whenever they put up a statue it's defaced… Bethnal Green is untidy, a pigsty.'

One of the most striking insights into the Bethnal Green psyche comes in fact from the nineteenth century. The opening of Bethnal Green's own museum in June 1872 gave rise to an interesting episode which saw Bethnal Greeners angrily asserting their right to be portrayed by journalists in a flattering way and not, as they saw it, misrepresented by the prejudices of their supposed social superiors. It is an interesting episode not least for underlining that sentimentality about the Bethnal Greeners was not always the projection of romantically-minded outsiders.

SLANDER

'And now, my friends, I ask you all, where were the horrid tribes
The dreadful set the Daily News and Telegraph describes
Could wretched boys and wretched girls such patriotism show
Would ugly hags with sinful face have welcomed Edward so ...
Could poor consumptive cripples, the hungry and the lean
Have danced as did the blooming girls and lads of Bethnal Green'

William Milton, *The Bethnal Green Slander*, 1872.

What became known as 'the Bethnal Green Slander' began with the ceremonial opening of the Bethnal Green Museum in June 1872. This was a highly charged event for East London. It was a Royal visit. It was also an occasion that expressed the country's new political mood following the suffrage reform of 1867 and the Education Act of 1870. To Bethnal Greeners, the sight of the Prince of Wales in the Bethnal Green Road must have been as strong a signifier of change as the new Board Schools beginning to erupt into the landscape.

The day was a triumph. The sun shone. There was a procession with military bands, an escort of Life Guards, horses and open carriages carrying grooms, equerries and Ladies of the Bed Chamber, bishops, peers and the Lord Mayor of London. The Prince was dressed in the red uniform of a general officer, the Princess 'in a pink bonnet and polonaise of the same colour, trimmed with point lace over a crimson petticoat'. Exotic touches were added by the presence among the official guests of a north American Indian chief in a ceremonial, embroidered blanket suit and a party from the Burmese embassy in white robes and gold vestments. Bethnal Green rose to the occasion with the route of the procession 'black with human ants', and 'planted thick with curious sightseers'. The men were in shirt sleeves and held long tobacco pipes, while 'the fairer sex was clad almost universally in cotton print frocks'. The cheering was deafening and the route was heavily decorated with flags, banners and home-made decorations. Deference and loyalty were both much in evidence on the banners, according to what was reported: 'Thank you for your kind visit. Long live Royalty, Science and Art. God bless the Prince and his Physician. Welcome to the East.'

This was an encounter between two sides of the metropolis, and the west stared at the east staring at the west. 'It was curious to observe the astonished gaze with which many of these people looked at the Life Guards and at Royalty,' mused one journalist. 'The constant exclamation "That's him, I know him by the pictures!" told the listener that thousands of the people of the metropolis had never seen the Prince before; and from their exclamations of admiration in respect of the Household troops "Ain't they fine" and "Ain't they beautiful" it was pretty clear that a field officer's escort of Life Guards was a scene which Bethnal Green had not witnessed within the memory of the oldest inhabitant.' The exclamations of the Prince and Princess were not recorded although it was certainly suggested that the feeling of astonishment was mutual. 'Until their visit to Bethnal Green they could scarcely have known much about that astonishing province in the empire of London, which is tenanted by an even more astonishing population, whose manners, customs, garbs and facial appearance seem to differ from those of the neighbours of north, south, east and west, as widely and as irreconcilably as Brittany differs from Bloomsbury.' The sense of difference was understandable. Many of the press accounts of the opening are riddled with metaphors of foreign travel and exploration, Bethnal Green being seen as 'terra incognita', a strange land of 'metropolitan orientals'. One journalist likened the Prince to Dr. Livingstone.

For many of the journalists the difference between east and west was portrayed as ranking or complement, rather than opposition. The fact of the Museum was taken as evidence of the happy truth that although differences existed between west and east, the two quarters were perfectly matched, like pieces in a jigsaw, and that both enjoyed the notional equality which nationhood bestowed on all sorts and conditions of men, irrespective of their obvious inequalities in life. The embodiment of this was of course the figure of the Prince and the rapturous reception, 'difficult to exaggerate', given to him by Bethnal Green was universally remarked on, as was the extrapolated political meaning. 'It is to be hoped,' said *The Times*, 'that it was witnessed by the handful of English Republicans who feel it in their duty to enter a protest against Royalty. If it was they must in their hearts feel that they have no followers among the masses of the English working classes'.

How were the East Enders themselves portrayed? Perhaps inevitably, many of the newspapers described for their readers a tribe of docile, deferential and long-suffering beings, whose poverty had somehow left their innate English qualities of politeness untouched. According to *The Times*, which waxed particularly sentimental about the character and conduct of the Bethnal Greeners, 'a better behaved multitude than that which assembled to see and cheer the Prince and Princess yesterday has never been gathered in any portion of the metropolis.' There was no sign of ruffianism but every sign of gratitude for the interest that had been taken in them: 'they are a grateful people'.

If this sentimentalised picture of the poor Bethnal Greeners was a construction of the west it was one in which the east willingly collaborated. In a letter to *The Times* a few days later, Septimus Hansard, the rector of Bethnal Green and one of the museum's local promoters, praised their coverage as being written 'in a kindly and truthful spirit', in contrast to the coverage in other papers. Hansard was voicing a feeling widely shared in Bethnal Green that wrong had been done to the district by some newspaper accounts of the day. The 'slander' provoked strong reactions.

Several 'indignation meetings' were held, during which newspaper accounts of the opening ceremony were read aloud. A boycott of the offending papers was organised.

Hansard was probably the author of a long letter which appeared in The *Echo* on July 6th under the pseudonym 'One of Them' and which explained the cause of Bethnal Green's grievance. 'We are represented as beings beyond the pale of humanity, unshapely phenomena… and the aristocratic visitors are, as it were, cautioned against the contamination of us monsters.' According to 'One of Them', the East was presented as a freak show at which the fashionable world might 'stop and laugh, and there is something intensely cruel in spurning us away when we come forward with extended hands and grateful hearts; in misrepresenting people who have but indifferent occasions of protesting, and assume their most cheerful look, their best appearance, to receive more worthily their wealthy countryman.'

What had caused such offence to be taken? The two culprits were the *Daily Telegraph* and the *Daily News,* and in both cases the offence was to concentrate on the inhabitants of the Old Nichol end of Bethnal Green, at that time of course a notorious slum. This patch of poverty was the first part of the East that the visitors from the West saw as they passed beyond the City's boundaries, and the journalists could not resist the temptation to melodramatise the scene. The *Daily Telegraph* had described the prince passing through 'dwarfs and hunchbacks, those creatures bent double, those crooked and bandy and rickety babes… Here yesterday female ugliness of face and form, in black monotonous unvarying typification was predominant. Sickly mothers nursing sickly babies; sickly girls toying in a sickly manner with sickly weaver boys, listless, emaciated middle-aged women; dreadful old women as ugly as sin, who looked as though they supported nature on a diet of Lucifer matches and gin.' The *Daily News* painted a picture of 'gaunt, ragged men, stunted narrow- chested, spider-limbed… of lean, wan-faced women, bareheaded in limp dingy prints, who as they cuddled to their breasts hydrocephalus infants, gazed in a kind of stunted amazement at the novel splendour.'

There are two ways of reading Bethnal Green's grievance at passages like these. One is a sense of wrong being done to the Old Nichol dwellers by such brutally frank portrayals. The other is the sense of wrong being done to the respectable Bethnal Greeners by lumping them in with such people. It was not so much the underlining of the distance between west and east that caused offence, it was the west's failure to recognise the distance between east-respectable, and east-residuum, a distance which should have kept east-respectable safely on the side of the national 'us' rather than the outcast 'them'.

The Bethnal Green slander burnt itself out within a few weeks but not before various broadsheets had been circulated. A lyric poem by William Milton expressed genteel outrage. A more brutal response came in a cartoon which rather undermined the Bethnal Greeners' claim to middle-class respectability by promising summary justice to the offending editors. Both are shown after a lynch mob had got to them and meted out a suitably robust Bethnal Green punishment, leaving two bodies swinging lifeless from a lamp post (see frontispiece). 'These caricatures,' said the *Echo* in justification of the rather startling image, 'roughly express the intense indignation of a set of people labouring under the sting of a false accusation'. It was 'the sarcasm' of the Liberal press that was to blame and not the bevahiour of the provoked. Indeed it was Bethnal Green who held the high moral ground '…and we hope that the time is not far off when, instead of receiving lessons in propriety from those who disdain us, we shall be enabled to offer them some'.

It was perhaps inevitable that the feelings of hurt stirred up by the perceived insult should turn into aggression against those who had so 'spurned' and 'disdained' them. For the Bethnal Green side, at least, it was a cruel lesson in the sour turn that romance can take, a lesson that unfortunately was to be repeated by the subsequent progress of the museum itself. In its opening week the new institution attracted over 50,000 visitors, a massive number of people which allowed all interested parties to claim success in bridge-building between the cultures of west and east. However, once the excitement had died down, the relationship between the two sides of the metropolis began to seem a little less happy.

2 BETHNAL GREEN AND NATIONAL MUSEUMS

'Why should the Imperial Exchequer maintain a local museum at Bethnal Green, the only place in the United Kingdom where it does so?
As far as I can see why should the Imperial Exchequer maintain South Kensington?
You cannot ask me questions; you must answer those addressed to you.'

Exchange between Sir John Gorst and Charles Barkworth Blow,
Select Committee on Museums of the Science and Art Department 1898.

The Bethnal Green slander was the first of many awkward episodes associated with the Bethnal Green Museum. The plain, brick-faced building that housed this accident-prone institution landed on a patch of land next to St John's Church in 1872, a talisman of change. The museum was nationally funded from the start and at the grand opening in 1872, sentiment-laden rhetoric filled the air. Much was said about education and national harmony. Alas, the dream of west and east coming together for mutual benefit soon vanished, leaving a legacy of disappointments, misunderstandings, broken promises and perceived injustices. To its critics the only object lesson the museum provided was one in false charity, whereby the rich gave to the poor but on the rich's terms and to their benefit. Visiting the museum a year after its opening, Henry James wrote gloomily of the hopelessness of its educational mission given the darkness and squalor that surrounded it. He doubted whether 'the haggard paupers of Bethnal Green' were in a fit state to feel any of the consolatory charm of art at all: 'for though art is an asylum, it is a sort of moated strong-hold, hardly approached save by some slender bridge-work of primary culture, such as the Bethnal Green mind is little practised in.' Walter Besant devoted a large part of a speech in 1887 to a scathing analysis of its failings: 'I have dwelt upon the Bethnal Green Museum at some length, not because I wished to attack the place, but because it seems to me an example of what ought not to be done.'

The 1898 Select Committee on Museums of the Science and Art Department offered an even more damning catalogue of evidence for the prosecution, describing with incredulity the bizarre objects laid before the people of Bethnal Green by their government in the name of education: the 700ft Japanese rope made of human hair, the large china negresses, the specimen jars of fibrine and

Left: 'The Eagle Slayer' by John Bell outside Bethnal Green Museum (installed 1872), 1994. Peter Marshall.

fat, the wax models of diseased meat, the art forgeries, the large scale model of a Spanish vineyard, the silver hansom cab and the ornately carved cabinets 'of vicious taste'. They heard evidence from the Bishop of Stepney that the museum was a 'lost opportunity'; from an LCC councillor that it was a 'white elephant'; and from one resident who lamented that 'there does not seem life, or energy or vitality about the thing at all … there is a sort of dead feeling; people seem to have forgotten the whole thing now and they take no interest in it'. The Committee concluded that the museum was little more than 'the rubbish heap of South Kensington' and a disgraceful waste of public money.

But if this was a white elephant it was one that carried fabulous treasure across cultural borders. Besides the permanent collections that so provoked the ire of its critics, the museum housed special exhibitions and these brought East the great private collections of the late nineteenth century. Sir Richard Wallace's collection of art treasures provided the opening exhibition in 1872. The Pitt-Rivers Collection, then known as Augustus Lane Fox's collection of anthropological specimens, was shown to the Bethnal Greeners from 1874 to 1878. The collection of national portraits lived in the Bethnal Green museum between 1885 and 1896 before finding a permanent home in a purpose-built gallery in the Charing Cross Road. Royal collections passed through: the Indian wedding presents of the Prince of Wales in 1876 and Queen Victoria's Jubilee presents in 1888. Less regal individuals who offered their property up to the gaze of the Bethnal Greeners included William Gladstone, whose collection of ivory was shown in 1875, Sir Cuthbert Quilter and Sir A.W. Franks, who exhibited his collection of oriental porcelain in 1875. Henry Willett's collection of ceramics was shown in 1899, followed by the English pottery and porcelain belonging to Mr and Mrs Salting. Lord Curzon's collection of oriental works of art remained at the Museum from 1906 until 1925. What did it all mean?

EDUCATION

'The most intristin'objek as it contains is, as far as we Bednal Grinners are consarned, the Hanimal Produks, as is a narrangmen'o' meets and t'other arktikls o'food, which is a rare an curus spectkl down about 'ere. Which we 'opes as the show will be hopen o' Sundays so as we might 'ave a belifool o'lookin' at meat if we ain't 'ad none for our dinners. Which is hoffen.'
The East London Museum by 'Our Bethnal Green-Grocer', *Punch*, 1872.

At its opening, the Bethnal Green Museum was hailed as a perfect fit between local and national, matching the surplus of the west with the need of the east. The Treasury had given the money for the project and the local parish had given the land on which the new museum sat. The building itself was a gift from national government in that it was the re-erected 'Brompton Boilers', transported from Hyde Park where the structure had housed the embryonic South Kensington Museum after the Great Exhibition. The railings used to fence off the plot of land were also government surplus and had also come from Hyde Park, where they had been torn down by the mob in the disorders of 1866. The state, in the shape of the Science and Art Department of the Committee of Council of Education, had given the new museum its core permanent collections. Bethnal Green was to provide the grateful people who were to look at the objects and learn from them.

The new museum was indeed a tale of two sides, a collaboration between two visions both of which had emerged from the post-Great Exhibition enthusiasm for creating 'metropolitan museums' to educate and improve the working population. The first vision was that the museum was to be a dynamic agent of social change in East London. In this dream, the swarm of one million impoverished worker bees east of Aldgate would be culturally, socially and economically reinvigorated by the nourishment provided by the new institution. This was the vision from a group of local men, led by Antonio Brady, a philanthropic admiralty official, and the Reverend Septimus Hansard, the rector of Bethnal Green. The second vision saw the new museum as the keystone of a national system of state museums, educational in character and matching the state-regulated design schools that the Department of Science and Art already controlled from South Kensington. This was the vision of the department's general superintendent, Henry Cole, whose unchallenged position of power gave the department its nickname of 'Cole's Kingdom'. Cole was a military man and saw virtue in the power of the state to bring order and efficiency to life.

The co-existence of two separate visions of the role and purpose of the museum was signalled at the opening by the apparent failure of the two parents to agree a name for their new offspring. To the local interest it was 'The East London Museum of Science and Art' but to the civil servants its official title was 'The Bethnal Green branch of the South Kensington Museum'. The difference in emphasis was significant and reflected not just the separate visions but also the separate paths which had led the two sides to the apparently happy wedding of the grand opening. Throughout the 1850s the flurry of thinking about metropolitan museums never strayed beyond the traditional assumptions of government that any such institutions were local affairs and should be paid for through local rates. But in the mid 1860s Antonio Brady moved East London's campaign for a metropolitan museum into a new arena of debate by suggesting that national government might legitimately engineer local improvement where self-help was impossible because of local impoverishment. Brady reinforced his argument by a clever proposal designed to lure government into treating East London as a special case. Under Brady's scheme, East London would give a plot of land to national government who would, 'in exchange for the site erect the building and maintain the museum'. The plot in question was a section of the 'Poor's Land', a triangular patch of open grazing land at the heart of Bethnal Green, owned by trustees and used since the seventeenth century to produce a small income for the local poor.

The Treasury was not impressed by Brady's offer and in December 1866 concluded that although the capital cost of any museum in Bethnal Green could be deemed legitimate expenditure, the ongoing revenue costs were definitely not: 'for they believe it to represent a policy inconsistent with the proper function of government and tending to open up an unlimited prospect of new claims upon the Public Exchequer', by which they meant 'other places throughout the United Kingdom whose inhabitants might be neither opulent nor public spirited enough to establish science and art museums, but who might still be glad to obtain them as free gifts from the Government'. Cole's department was, however, in bullish mood and countered the Treasury's objections with a completely new argument. Setting aside any educational benefit to the local population, the new museum was important to the government on purely practical grounds: it was desirable to accept Brady's offer of land 'in order that a museum should be erected and maintained there at the public cost to hold certain collections, being national property, which occupy space now urgently required for more pressing purposes'. The pressing purposes were the rapidly growing art collections at South Kensington. The 1860s was a period of enthusiastic and unrestrained collecting on the part of the department's officials who focussed their efforts almost exclusively on fine and decorative arts: French furniture, Italian majolica, silver and paintings. As the space needs for the newly purchased art exhibits grew, so too did the problem of finding somewhere else to house the older collections of non-art objects. Although unwanted in South Kensington, these objects were nevertheless national property and therefore unable to be disposed of.

As discussions about the Bethnal Green project continued, creating growing friction between the Treasury and Cole, the definition of the new museum's purpose was rephrased. It was to be 'a national institution for the reception and exhibition of objects of science and art being national property, which are insufficiently provided for elsewhere'. But essentially the justification for national funding rested on the state's practical need to accommodate its surplus property, rather than any desire to educate its workers. Housing objects 'insufficiently provided for elsewhere', with its vague associations of removing impediments to progress, became the favoured phrase from the South Kensington side, and no opportunity was lost to cast the notion in a positive light. Henry Cole went furthest in turning necessity into virtue by claiming that 'a principle in the scheme of metropolitan museums was that each should have a distinguishing characteristic and not merely degenerate into second-rate replicas of earlier established national museums in the metropolis'. In other words, it was to Bethnal Green's benefit that the main museum in South Kensington should keep the art treasures and Bethnal Green should have the left-overs, curios and oddities. Although the Department of

Science and Art always claimed to be the flourishing and progressive force of educational good, as opposed to the reactionary force of propertied interest, as exemplified by the British Museum and other such institutions run by trustees, the Bethnal Green episode revealed that even in Cole's kingdom, property always trumped education. From the South Kensington point of view, the museum in Bethnal Green was all about us rather than them.

The idea that the museum was primarily a store for unwanted national property was not mentioned at the opening in 1872. Speeches presented the institution as the triumphant development of South Kensington's educational mission to provide technical education for artisans and to improve the taste and enlightenment of the general public. Only the *Saturday Review* sounded a more cynical note. The location of the new museum was grudgingly seen as a move in the right direction: 'this would seem to be but poor and tardy compensation for the policy which South Kensington has persistently and perseveringly pursued, of removing all the museums and collections it can lay hands on to as great a distance as possible from the masses of the people.' The exhibits, however, were criticized. 'South Kensington has done nothing for its protégée except start it in the world with a dusty collection of stale pickles which is supposed to convey a vivid idea of the chemical analysis of food.' The pickles referred to the Food Collection, one of two discrete collections that were transferred to the Bethnal Green museum as the core of its educational content. The other was the Animal Products Collection. None of South Kensington's newly acquired art objects were sent to Bethnal Green, although this absence was initially masked by the presence of Sir Richard Wallace's paintings and furniture, temporarily loaned to Bethnal Green for a mixture or reasons, but generally perceived to be fulfilling a broadly educational function. 'He has chosen the East End for the exhibition … particularly that the poor furniture makers who abound in that neighbourhood will gain many valuable hints from the articles he shows connected with that industry.' Wallace's treasures were removed from Bethnal Green within two years, leaving the educational mission of the new museum resting solely on its curious exhibits related to animals and food.

The Animal Products Collection was one of many formed in the aftermath of the Great Exhibition. An initiative of the Society of Arts, it was intended to fill the gap between the collections of minerals and vegetables already established as the Museum of Practical Geology, housed in Jermyn Street, and the Museum of Economic Biology, housed at Kew. Both these collections were already government-owned. The Animal Products joined them when the collection was bought by the Royal Commissioners for the Exhibition of 1851 and presented to the government, together with other property to the value of £14,000. On the opening of the South Kensington Museum in June 1857, the collection was exhibited in its entirety, alongside a number of other miscellaneous collections formed in the post-Great Exhibition collecting craze. But as art came to dominate South Kensington, so animal products moved to the margins and in 1862 both it and the Naval Architecture Collection were re-housed elsewhere on the South Kensington site. In 1872 it was dispatched to Bethnal Green.

The collection had something of the character of a literary and philosophical cabinet of curiosities from an earlier generation. Examples of silk worms, sea shells, ivory, bone, fur and feathers, shared showcases with samples of textiles and leather in finished form. It included curiosities such as a 700ft long rope made in Japan from female hair which was stated to have taken nearly 5 years to make and to have used up the hair of an entire province of women 'shorn of their locks in obedience to a mandate issued by the Government of the Tycoon in 1859'. At Bethnal Green it sat alongside another quasi-scientific oddity: the Museum of Economic Entomology formed by Dr Andrew Murray, a one time secretary of the Royal Horticultural Society. This consisted of wax models of insects.

The Food Collection was a later initiative. Formed in 1857 by Thomas Twining of Twickenham, it was intended to help establish 'an Economic Museum that should compromise illustrations of every-day life for the working classes'. Despite its origin with a private individual, the collection had been developed within the state framework by Lyon Playfair, the chemist who for a brief period in the 1850s held joint office with Henry Cole and formed a rival centre of power to Cole's monarchy. Playfair resigned in 1857 leaving the science-related collections, including food, without a champion. However, the collection's didactic character was preserved. 'The Food Collection,' said the museum guidebook, 'has been arranged with the express object of teaching the nature and sources of the food which rich and poor alike need for the maintenance of their daily life.'

The food exhibits did indeed make up a rare and curious spectacle. They included supposedly instructional groups, such as pickle jars containing the 'fibrine, fat and other constituents of the human body', typological specimens of dried foreign breads, such as Dikka bread from the Gabon and 'strange objects considered as delicacies by other nations', represented by sea slugs and edible birds' nests. Wax models were plentiful, according to the catalogue. 'Diseased meat. Model in wax of a piece of diseased pork called "measeled pork"; horse tongue modelled in wax. exhibited for comparison with a bullock's tongue also modelled in wax and shown with it.' One of the most popular exhibits was a wax representation of the normal day's rations for a prisoner in Pentonville Jail. The collection also relied heavily on gifts from manufacturers, who presumably saw the advertising advantages of presenting their products to the public as educational object lessons: 'Preserved Meats. Examples of a preparation called Fluid Meat – presented by Messers Darby and Gosden, 140 Leadenhall St. London EC'; 'a variety of steam-made biscuits manufactured from wheaten flour – Exhibited by Messrs Peak Frean & Co. Dockhead, Bermondsey'. Fortnum and Mason supplied 'almonds, comfits, candy and a variety of table ornaments made of sugar'. The collection also contained 'many interesting diagrams' demonstrating, for example, 'the relative amounts of sugar, tea, tobacco consumed by the population of various countries'. There were comparative tables showing 'the quantity of matter daily wasted – and therefore requiring to be daily supplied … by the soldier, the refined lady and the hearty schoolboy,' and 'the various nutritive values of vegetables.' The latter, according to the guide book, assigned the lowest value to 'the indigestible cucumber, thus fully justifying the sentence of the old physician, that the last process in preparing it for consumption ought to consist in throwing it out of the window.'

These collections were considered at the time to be 'educational' and 'instructive', but what exactly were they meant to convey and to whom? There is little evidence of much critical self-analysis at the Department of Science and Art beyond an absolute conviction that their museums were educational and therefore quite different from the British Museum, which, it was said, was 'quite opposed to the purpose of instruction which informs South Kensington'. Despite the absence of reflection, the tone and content of most of South Kensington's pronouncements about education suggest that its officers never moved far from the utilitarian and mechanistic end of the educational spectrum. They saw their duty as exposing officially validated articles to the gaze of the people and presenting these articles in a structured arrangement. Any understanding that resulted was largely the responsibility of the individual, although the department would offer some help by making its useful knowledge further available through the medium of catalogues. Overall, the museum project was an exercise in standard-setting and official information. This of course matched the department's approach to art education, a process dominated by the act of copying.

Seeing South Kensington's role as primarily one of standard-defining helps to explain the frustration felt by those whose definition of education included some element of interaction between teacher and pupil. Walter Besant argued that merely showing things was not enough, it left the Bethnal Green museum as '… a dumb and silent gallery. One may compare it to a Board School newly built, provided with all the latest appliances for education – with books, desks, seats, blackboards, and everything, including crowds of pupils, but left without a teaching staff, the pupils being expected to teach themselves.' Besant also poured scorn on the science and art department's fundamental assumption, which was that objects alone would give object lessons. 'Here, says the Department, is the Bethnal Green Museum with its doors wide open: let the people walk in and inspect the contents. So, if we invited the people to inspect a collection of cuneiform inscriptions, we might just as well expect them to carry away a knowledge of Assyrian history: or by exhibiting an electrical machine we might as well expect them to understand the appliances of electricity. It is not enough, in fact, to exhibit pictures: they must be explained. It is with paintings and drawings as with everything else. The visitors to a museum are

Overleaf: Frieze by F.W. Moody on the Bethnal Green Museum (1872), 2006. Peter Marshall.

like travellers in a foreign country, of whom Emerson truly says that when they leave, they take nothing away but what they brought with them.'

By the time Besant was writing, Sir Richard Wallace's art treasures had long since been returned to central London but art had begun to have a presence in the permanent collections as the department began to transfer some of its own furniture and decorative arts to Bethnal Green. This, to the Museum's critics, added insult to injury in that the exhibits sent east were not ones from which local furniture makers should learn. The timing of Bethnal Green's opening could not have been worse in this respect. The early 1870s marked a sea-change in taste as artistic fashion turned its back on the florid opulence of the 1850s and embraced sparer, aesthetic styles. South Kensington officials had purchased enthusiastically at the Great Exhibition of 1851, its successor the International Exhibition of 1862 and the Paris Exhibition of 1867, the latter with a not-insubstantial parliamentary vote of money. All three initiatives had acquired for the nation a collection of modern furniture and decorative objects embodying the rich and heavily sophisticated French workmanship that was so admired in the middle of the century. Within 10 years these styles had fallen so much from favour in artistic circles that the objects themselves were considered as dangers to public health: they were 'poisonous' and 'vicious', the deployment of ornament in such ostentatious abundance was 'wicked'.

The 1898 Select Committee found it significant that all of these 'undesirable objects' had found their way to Bethnal Green and pressed department officials hard on the question of why Bethnal Green rather than South Kensington should be the home of the pottery statues of negresses, ornately inlaid cabinets and massively carved sideboards, particularly two by Wright & Mansfield and Fourdinois, both prize-winners at Paris in 1867. The presence of these objects was unjustifiable in the view of the committee who recommended that 'the furniture should be replaced by examples which the local people might copy without risking their livelihood'. The questionable artistic merit of the objects at Bethnal Green was not denied by Caspar Purdon Clarke, then the Director of Art at South Kensington, who admitted that the furniture had 'no teaching value', as far as art was concerned, but offered the excuse that their value was 'historical rather than artistic'. When pressed as to why this wasn't explained fully on the labels, he offered the evasive reply that judgments about artistic merit rested only on differences of opinion and in any case 'some people prefer the Wright and Mansfield cabinet to Poynter and Burgess'. Sir John Donnelly, Cole's successor, later added another shaky justification, which was that although the profusely carved 1860s furniture was not 'to the taste of the day', the decoration 'would furnish in its innumerable details motives of greater use to an art workman than a specimen of purer outline'.

By 1898 virtually all of South Kensington's modern manufactured objects had been dispatched to Bethnal Green, following, it was said, a decision made in the early 1880s.

This marked a significant move on the part of the science and art department away from what had been in the 1850s one of its defining principles, the acquisition of modern manufacturers: 'I may be wrong,' said Richard Redgrave to the 1873 committee investigating the transfer of the South Kensington empire to the British Museum's trustees, 'but I believe that the British Museum purchases with a totally different view from ours. Our view is the advancement of taste, especially in manufactures. I can conceive that the British Museum would say "What do you buy these modern things for? What do you buy furniture made in modern times for?" ' By 1914 the department had shifted to the opposite view and what was by then the Victoria and Albert Museum, had re-focussed its collecting almost wholly on the decorative arts of the past, allowing the direct link between manufacturers and museum to wither, despite the rearrangement of the displays in 1908, ostensibly to make the museum more useful to workmen. By 1914 it was openly admitted that the whole industrial art museum initiative had failed. 'After 50 years of experiment,' said Cecil Smith, South Kensington's Director of Museums, in response to a proposal for a new museum of industrial art, 'it can hardly be denied that the object aimed at has not been attained... the result is a growing discontent and the gap between South Kensington, on the one hand, and the manufacturers and the buying public, on the other, goes on widening.' Bethnal Green had long provided embarrassing evidence that the gap between the state's museums and the state's workforce was no less wide in the east of London as it was in the west.

If Bethnal Green failed to provide object lessons in art for workmen, did it succeed in providing information about diet and healthy eating for the general public? Some exhibits certainly offered practical tips. 'A poor man's filter is exhibited in the Museum,' pointed out the guidebook helpfully, 'which can be very easily and cheaply constructed by using a common flower pot, glazed inside, plugging the drainage hole (not too tightly) with a piece of clean sponge, then adding layers of animal, charcoal, sand and rather coarse gravel.' Despite the odd helpful hint, the food exhibits were displayed in Playfair's original typological arrangement and thus presented as a lesson in science and chemistry rather than diet. In the 1898 Select Committee John Burns pressed Sir John Donnelly on whether this was appropriate. 'You surely would admit that 50 or 60 cases of chemical analysis of oats and wheat and barley and carrots and turnips and vegetables are not the most interesting objects to place before a population of the character of the East End of London, say, out for a Bank Holiday?' Donnelly conceded that he didn't suppose they were. Another witness to the 1898 committee believed that they 'do not do an atom of good to anyone unless to persuade them to take in some vegetarian lectures'. To Henry James in 1872, the food exhibits could not be taken as other than 'irritating from a Bethnal Green, that is a hungry, point of view'.

After Bethnal Green there was no more talk of metropolitan museums or a Cole-style network of national institutions, although the idea vaguely lived on in the V&A's circulation department which lent exhibits from South Kensington to municipal museums elsewhere in the country. The idea of a nationally funded school of art and design in East London also faded. The matter of the missing school had been raised in Parliament in 1873 and 1885 but to no avail. In the 1890s a serious attempt by the Technical Education Board of the London County Council to revive the original vision for Bethnal Green and create an educational centre of excellence around the museum also failed. After 50 ignominious years of educational under-achievement, the 1920s saw a genuine attempt to turn Bethnal Green into a model educational museum, but this time for children. The initiative was based on up-to-date thinking and resulted in child-friendly natural history exhibits introduced into the displays. However local interests continued to take second place to the interests of the museum's South Kensington parent: as witness the Victoria and Albert Museum's 'modern collections', whose downwards spiral in status was eventually halted by changing fashion. As interest in nineteenth and twentieth-century design rose in the 1960s, so too did cries for the modern collections to 'return home' to South Kensington, 'to be wholeheartedly displayed in the Victoria and Albert, instead of tucked away in the gloom of Bethnal Green'. There had been no such reprieve for the food and the animal products collections which had both spiralled downwards to the point of no return. By the early 1920s the food exhibits had been condemned and were awaiting disposal; the animal products had become infested with moths and were also recommended for 'urgent disposal'.

PROPERTY

'On my last visit to this museum, for instance, I chanced upon two women who were standing before a vase. It was a large and very beautiful vase, of admirable form and proportions and it was decorated on the top by a group representing three captives chained to the rock. Their comment on the work of art was as follows: "Look", said one 'look at those poor men chained to the rock." "Yes", said the other, "poor fellows. Ain't it shocking".'
Walter Besant, 1884.

If the Bethnal Green Museum failed to educate the Bethnal Greeners in what was good in art or food, what other sort of object lesson did the museum provide? Here, it is worth turning to the other exhibits that were sent east for the appreciation of the people: the private collections. Following the lead set by Sir Richard Wallace, many philanthropically minded individuals offerd up their prized possessions to be exposed to the gaze of the Bethnal Green public: Queen Victoria, Colonel Lane Fox (later Pitt-Rivers), William Gladstone and Lord Curzon among them.

These private collections make a striking contrast to the collections owned by the state. If the latter were tumbling down the spiral of cultural status, the former were rapidly rising, and their passage through Bethnal Green appears to have speeded the ascent. There is no reason to doubt the philanthropic spirit that moved the wealthy to lend their possessions. However, it is undeniable that such demonstrations did reap rewards. In the case of Richard Wallace, his objects subsequently passed into public ownership. The Wallace Collection opened as a national museum at Hertford House in London's West End in June 1900, in accordance with the wishes of Wallace's widow, whose will had specified that the site of the Wallace Collection should be 'in a central part of London'. The Pitt-Rivers Collection also went into semi-public ownership. After its showing at Bethnal Green it was subsequently transferred to the main South Kensington Museum where it had a lukewarm reception and in 1883 was offered to, and accepted by, the University of Oxford. Wallace's property is now a treasured part of Britain's national heritage, as are the objects collected by A.W. Franks and George Salting, which together constitute a large part of the British Museum and Victoria and Albert Museum's holdings of ceramics. The process whereby collections passed through the gateway of Bethnal Green on their way to a Valhalla elsewhere was repeated on a smaller scale for Henry Willett, whose collection is now one of the treasures of Brighton Museum and Art Gallery, and Lord Curzon, whose collection is now displayed at Keddleston Hall in Derbyshire.

The drawing together of national museums and wealthy connoisseurs at the end of the nineteenth century is a fascinating story. However when seen in the context of the national museum in Bethnal Green, and its failure to deliver its promised educational mission, the story is a slightly uncomfortable one. Despite the rhetoric of bringing the two sides of the nation together, didn't the juxtaposition of fabulous possessions and poor people achieve the opposite by underlining differences. In July 1872 an episode offered the Bethnal Greeners an unambiguous object lesson in the social privileges accorded to wealth. In that month W.E. Forster, the Vice-President of the Education Office, was asked in the House of Commons whether he was aware that any visitors had been admitted to the Bethnal Green Museum last Sunday. The significance of this question was that the arrival of the museum had placed a new focus on the question of Sunday opening, long a source of irritation in connection with the British Museum, considering that Sunday was the one day of leisure when working men and women might visit. Forster was forced to admit that Cole had agreed 'on his own responsibility in accordance with previous custom, to issue chiefly to Peers and members of the House of Commons tickets of admission to the museum available for Sunday afternoon'. Sir Richard Wallace had also been issued with a ticket on the grounds that it would be wrong to prevent him inspecting his own paintings. Forster reassured the House that the practice was to be stopped. 'Whatever might be our own personal opinions in regard to the general policy of opening museums on Sundays, there can be little doubt that the Bethnal Green Museum should not be opened to the rich and closed to the poor on that day.'

The museum created striking contrasts between the worlds of rich and poor on every level. Although contemporary accounts of the private collections are always sprinkled with the notion that the loan was somehow instructional or improving to the Bethnal Greeners, there is very often an overt acknowledgement that the exhibits were little more than superficial diversions. The *Illustrated London News* reported the arrival of Wallace's collections as 'a gratifying occasion for the poor people of that rather shabby and depressed quarter. It needs to be cheered now and then with the display of beautiful objects, if nothing can be done for the revival of its industrial prosperity'. For several critics, the only transmissible messages detected in the objects, were vague notions of improvement and self-help, inspired by the heroism of the connoisseur-philanthropist.

One private collection which arrived in Bethnal Green with explicit instructional intentions towards the Bethnal Greeners was the Pitt-Rivers Collection. Its creator, Colonel A.H. Lane Fox, was a passionate advocate of museums. Like Cole, he had no doubts about his mission. 'I hold that the great desideratum of our day is an educational museum in which the visitor may instruct themselves… We have placed power in the hands of the masses and the masses are ignorant and knowledge is swamped by ignorance.' He had no sympathy with the British Museum ('only in a molluscous and invertebrate condition of development'). The South Kensington Museum he considered to be a specialist technical museum and 'not a museum for general educational purposes, as it can never have been contemplated that the whole or the majority of visitors should qualify as manufacturers or artists'. Lane Fox had grand ambitions for his collection: it was amassed 'solely with a view to instruction' and the knowledge his objects was intended to convey was 'the succession of ideas by which the minds of men in a primitive condition of culture have progressed from the simple to the complex and from the homogeneous to the heterogeneous'.

The display of his highly-charged collection in the context of 1870s East London created many resonances. This was a time of new ideas: the London dockers were beginning to flex their collective muscles, the casual poor were beginning to loom large in middle-class fears, science was starting to organise charity. Lane Fox saw his creation as illustrating social change proceeding as a gradual and moderate process of evolution, rather than revolution. He saw it illustrating the impossibility of intercourse between 'two nations in very different stages of civilisation brought side to side'. He saw it as demonstrating that progress was a single path 'progress is like a game of dominoes – like fits onto like'. How were these object lessons received by the people of Bethnal Green? Alas, we can only speculate. One of the few formal records of a response from a member of the public is found in a letter from the museum to Lane Fox in September 1874 informing him, with regret, that 'five small darts attached to the Bengal blow pipe were taken away on Saturday evening last… it is supposed by a visitor.'

One can also only speculate about the deeper messages received by the people of Bethnal Green when faced with the other inspirational displays of heroic property ownership. But the speculation is intriguing. If Bethnal Green failed in its educational aspirations of instructing people about art, food and animal products, did it in fact succeed in transmitting a clear message about the redemptive powers of property. Was this in fact the common ground which us and them both settled on as a comfortable arena in which to conduct their courtship. Bethnal Green, like most poor areas, was an area where property was accorded much significance, a fact well in evidence on the day of the museum's opening. The west brought to the east the private property of Sir Richard Wallace: objects of fabulous value such as Sèvres porcelain, gilt bronze candelabra and works by Leonardo da Vinci. In return the east welcomed its visitors from the west with a public display of their own property. 'The householders simply stripped their rooms of the most showy objects they contained and stuck them up outside. Old rugs, carpets, curtains, tea trays, chimney-piece ornaments and fireplace finery in tissue paper were all included in this frank and homely system of embellishment. Here and there a shopkeeper had come out strong with crimson-cloth and Dutch-metal; but the most significant and touching feature of the scene was the sincerity with which the people produced their simple, domestic contribution to the general display.'

Several journalists witnessing the day remarked on the 'fondness among the Metropolitan orientals for bright colours and picturesque pomp', and this does raise the thought that the Bethnal Green Museum was, perhaps, a more natural fit with its local community than its promoters on either side imagined. The presence of an institution where the state, the Crown and some of the country's most wealthy individuals all underlined the importance of owning household goods with conspicuously florid ornament could perhaps be seen as a statement of common values. In 1883 a journalist for *Cassell's Family Magazine* reported with some amusement the behaviour of the Bethnal Greeners when faced with a display of valuable ceramics. 'The visitors round about us were expressing their comments upon those freely enough and in tones sufficiently audible. "Lor!" cried one young girl to her gaily dressed companion indicating with outstretched finger a large earthenware vase of Italian manufacture, "If we ain't got just sich another jug as that at 'ome".' What was amusing to the journalist was perhaps a more telling indication of the museum's topsy-turvy success. If the Bethnal Green Museum failed in its educational mission of providing a lighthouse for art and science in East London, perhaps it succeeded in bringing the two halves of the nation together in more mysterious ways. And if so, the common value that the museum preached was surely property: property as the main definer of social status and the chief criteria of citizenship.

Overleaf: Shop in Seabright Street, 1993. Peter Marshall.

3 BETHNAL GREEN AND THE ENGLISH CRAFTSMAN

'A man came yesterday from Bethnal Green with an account of that district. They are all weavers, forming a kind of separate community. There they are born, there they live and die… They are for the most part out of employment and can get none: 1,100 are crammed into the poor house, 5 or 6 in a bed, 6,000 receive parochial relief… The district is in a complete state of insolvency and hopeless poverty.'

Charles Greville, 17 February 1832.

The story of the East London silk weavers is one of nineteenth-century London's most distressing tales. It was *par excellence* a tale of two sides with the unfortunate 'them' pushed far beyond the pale by location, condition and occupation. 'By mid-century silk weaving was synonymous with poverty and Bethnal Green, the centre of the trade, was the poorest district in London', as David Green, a writer on metropolitan pauperism, summarises it. But this is also a tale about empathy and coming together, at least on the sentimental level. It is less about the definition of outcast London as its redemption. The more the weavers were cast out, the more they seemed to belong, personifying a thoroughly Christian insider story of virtue and suffering. As the nineteenth century progressed, so the 'separate community' of weavers in Bethnal Green became caught up in new ways of understanding English society as an organic, holistic thing, a body which could ill afford to think of itself as separate parts. And, as always with Bethnal Green, it was location that gave the place power to move the middle-class imagination. The tragedy being played out before middle-class Londoners' eyes in the middle of the nineteenth century could not be dismissed as an episode perpetrated at a distance by savage northerners. It was much closer to home. The parish of Bethnal Green was the failed state in the heart of the capital. As it descended into an ever more terrible hell of chaos, filth and suffering, so it conjured up the spectre of national failure as well as local.

Many occupational groups in nineteenth-century England provided evidence of the country's effortless ability to create paupers as a by-product of creating wealth. What made the Bethnal Green weavers particularly compelling witnesses to the dark side of national progress was their distinctive set of attributes and associations.

Left: Pereira Street, c. 1900.

Above all, there was the product they made: silk. This most aristocratic of fabrics was the stuff of kings and queens, an association which gave the weavers enormous symbolic capital. 'I'm sure if the ladies who wears what we makes, or the Queen of England herself, was to see our state, she'd never let her subjects suffer such privations in the land of plenty,' said one weaver, as reported by Mayhew. The beauty of silk added to the poignancy of the weavers' plight. Many newspaper accounts of the conditions in which the pauper weavers lived dwelt on the fairy-tale contrast between the beautiful, shimmering fabric and the wretched surroundings from which it came. Mayhew, for example, described 'an exquisite piece of maroon-coloured velvet, that amidst the squalor of the place seemed marvellously beautiful and it was a wonder to find it unsoiled amidst the filth that surrounded it'. The weavers were rather more than just another group of troublesome artisans, they played a part in national ritual and there was a magic about their skills.

The second thing that made the weavers so compelling was the degree of their degradation, specifically the filth in which they lived. The archetypal description of conditions in Bethnal Green was published in 1848 by the sanitary reformer Hector Gavin, a stomach-churning account of foulness inside and out. Others came after him and as conditions deteriorated further, Bethnal Green became the site for texts visceral to the point of scatological pornography as journalists lavishly described the feel and smells of a place liquid with black slime, where human beings lived out their lives between putrid heaps of decomposing waste and in cellars damp with sewage. The descriptions of mid-century Bethnal Green have an elemental force, often made more powerful by the fact that the human beings placed in this vision of a foetid black hell are semi-clothed or naked.

The Bethnal Green weavers also had compelling Christian credentials in their perceived Protestant genealogy. Many were indeed descended from Huguenot refugees (although in truth just as many were descended from Irish Catholics) and the newspaper articles often present the semi-naked women and children in rags as figures of essential sanctity and Christian virtue brought low by forces beyond their control. Christian resonances echoed through much of the agonizing about the weavers at the height of their distress and continued to sound after the London silk industry's effective death by 1900. Those few weavers who survived underwent a remarkable apotheosis after death, the nineteenth century's wretched man of sorrow being resurrected as the twentieth century's robust English craftsman, a symbol of national continuity enshrining the people's innate mechanical ingenuity and the enduring Protestant work ethic.

If this is a story of the growth of empathy and brotherhood between two sides, it also a rather one-sided one. The debate in this chapter is less between Bethnal Green and the outside world as between various opinions from the outside world about what the weavers' plight actually meant. The Bethnal Green weavers were in many ways all-purpose icons, adaptable to all shades of nineteenth-century opinion as it underwent its long bout of self-analysis. Did the weavers represent the sad but inevitable casualties of national progress as free trade evangelists ushered in a better economic system. Or did they demonstrate that this new economic system was a false god and incompatible with Christian values? As the idea of handicrafts came to prominence towards the end of the century, did the weavers signify a possible future for London's economic prosperity? If so, what sort of nation did they represent: the socialism of the progressive end of the Arts and Crafts movement or a more traditional hierarchy of class and caste. Did the weavers speak of the poor man at the gate or the rich man in his castle? If opinions differed about what exactly the weaver stood for, so too did views on how to restore him and the nation to health. Those of a Christian bent called for medicine; those of a utilitarian bent called for surgery, most notoriously Richard Cobden, with his comment 'let the silk trade perish'. The never-disputed fact was that the weavers in Bethnal Green were suffering terribly as a consequence of whatever was happening.

SILK

'Twas August and the fierce sun overhead
Smote on the squalid streets of Bethnal Green,
And the pale weaver, through his window seen
In Spitalfields, look'd thrice dispirited.'

Matthew Arnold, from the sonnet East London, 1850.

The plight of the East London weavers in the nineteenth century was a story that unfolded in public through the pages of newspapers and magazines. From the 1820s onwards, *The Times* is littered with references to Bethnal Green, rising to an intensity in the twenty years between 1840 and 1860. The picture that emerges from these accounts is of a terrible place whose inhabitants were sinking into a black quicksand of distress, starvation, suicide, disease and death. The weavers were indeed, in Matthew Arnold's words, thrice dispirited: their livelihood had gone, they were living in beastly conditions and they had no hope of salvation because their local welfare systems had failed. Alongside the tales of human tragedy at the local scale, the newspapers also rehearsed the national arguments that such misery represented. Chief amongst these was the debate surrounding free trade, the fiscal policy so bound up with the weavers' fate. The declining fortunes of the weavers were inextricably entangled with the rising doctrines of the political economists. The milestones in the decline of London's silk industry were the very same landmark events that 'liberated' Britain from its old protectionist legislation and ushered in the supposedly healthier but far harsher world of *laissez-faire*.

The production of silk cloth by hand-loom weaving had been a boom industry of the eighteenth century, a natural consequence of London's population surge and the demand for fashionable cloth that came with it. The weaving industry had settled in Spitalfields, to the east of the City, initially a consequence of the migration of French Huguenot weavers fleeing religious persecution. In 1680 there was one French Protestant church in the City of London: by 1700 there were nine. By the mid-eighteenth century the numbers of weavers in Spitalfields had swelled massively with the arrival of hand-loom weavers from the north of England and Ireland, pulled into the metropolis by the magnetic attraction of easy money. As more weavers arrived, so the weaving district spread eastwards from Spitalfields, creating new roads, new buildings and, in 1746, the new parish of Bethnal Green. Interestingly, even at the birth of the parish questions were raised over its viability as a unit, given that the journeyman weavers who were to form it could barely sustain themselves let alone a parish administration system.

As the eighteenth century turned to the nineteenth, the number of looms at work in the eastern district had multiplied and the weavers had barricaded themselves into their trade with a formidable network of regulations, import duties and price-fixing to protect their livelihoods. But the bubble had already burst. Competition came from two quarters. French silk, generally acknowledged to be finer in quality, took the top end of the market: cheaper English silk, produced at lower cost on the new power looms in the Midlands and North, began to squeeze the bottom end. The London industry was caught in the middle and by 1830 the 25,000 looms at work in the metropolis in 1824 had been reduced to 14,000. By 1860 numbers had shrunk to 8,000 and by 1900 under 100 were left. Despite an enlightened attempt to transplant the industry into more sustainable factory conditions with the foundation in Bethnal Green of the East London Silk Mill in 1870, the collapse was total. The 7,847 weavers recorded in Bethnal Green in 1838 had disappeared by the time of the 1901 census leaving only 548 people employed in the weaving trade in the whole of London. The more fortunate of Bethnal Green's former weavers became publicans and costermongers, the less fortunate died as paupers. The firm who had led the factory venture, Warner & Sons, moved out of London in 1895 to the cleaner air of Braintree, taking their weavers with them and leaving the hand-looms behind. In 1919 silk production at Braintree was turned over wholly to power looms. By 1921 when Frank Warner wrote his history of the silk industry, the London trade was represented by 114 elderly hand-loom silk weavers, all working on ancient looms in the top front rooms of their terrace cottages in Bethnal Green, supplying six London merchants with small pieces of silk for ties and head scarves. By the outbreak of the second world war only eleven weavers were left.

Looked at with hindsight, the nature of the London silk industry's collapse seems relatively straightforward. In his 1939 *History of East London*, Hubert Llewellyn Smith advanced two reasons for the London trade's failure to make the transition to modern economic conditions. It was an exotic manufacture, and therefore vulnerably dependent on foreign sources for its raw materials; it had taken root in a place where local conditions did not favour the development of factory-based production. The particular form of industrial revolution that had swelled London's textile trades in the eighteenth century relied not on steam power but on outwork, which by the nineteenth century translated into sweating: 'the weavers entered on a prolonged but hopeless struggle by means of long hours and low earnings to make head against the formidable competition of outside areas'. Added to these two basic handicaps was the ascendancy of new economic doctrines which, in the name of free trade, cut away the protective duties and regulations that had sustained hand-loom weaving in the eighteenth century. Silk was targeted by the political economists as a particularly tightly trussed example of an alien and artificially sustained trade. Not only did it operate with protective duties against foreign imports, but it also protected itself through 'the Spitalfields Acts' which regulated wages and thus impeded the healthy flow of capital and ingenuity. Accordingly, in William Huskisson's evangelical free trade budget of 1824 the Spitalfields Acts were repealed and two years later restrictions on imported silk were loosened. The final nail in the coffin came in 1860 when Cobden 'set the trade free' entirely by removing all import duties, with predictably devastating consequences. 'Let the silk trade perish' was Cobden's notorious comment. In his 1921 history Frank Warner, called the years between 1860 and 1890 the black decades, but pointedly sidestepped any allocation of blame: 'it is not the object of this work to attempt to prove that our past or present fiscal policy has been either the salvation or the ruin of the silk industry in this country. The facts must be left to speak for themselves.'

To evangelical economists of the 1830s, the individual distress of the weavers was an unfortunate but marginal consequence of national progress: proof that the hard medicine of free trade was working. Some even suggested that the removal of duties had strengthened the trade. G.R. Porter, for example, wrote an account of silk weaving in the 1830s which painted a rosy picture of the post-Huskisson weaver, happily at work with his family, all usefully employed, orderly and cheerful. Frank Warner, in 1921, noted that this account was 'in singular contrast to most of the gloomy ones of the time and, though evidently true to life, was such as could have been but rarely been found at the time'. The economist Henry Parnell in 1831 admitted that the trade had become depressed but placed the blame on the weavers and their over-production, rather than foreign competition: '... on the whole, it may be stated in the most unqualified language, that it is a false inference to draw from the distress which did prevail some time ago in these manufactures, that the alteration of the laws in 1825 was instrumental in producing it'.

To the Benthamites, the weavers' misfortunes were entirely self-imposed. Witnesses to several parliamentary enquiries of the 1830s attached blame to their clannishness and unhealthy refusal to circulate their labour. 'The weavers are strongly attached to the locality in which they have become accustomed and rarely if ever think of a market for their labour by removing to a distant part.' Their 'feebleness as a race' was also noted: 'that the weavers of Spitalfields are of small stature has long been a matter of public notoriety'; 'they are decayed in their bodies, the whole race of them is rapidly descending to the size of Lilliputians'. In his evidence to the 1835 Royal Commission on education Francis Place called them '… a physically degraded people. There were no tall men among them. Their manners are coarser than that of any other tradesman.' Blame was also attached to the quality of their work: it was the weavers' own fault that their silk was inferior to French. As early as 1747 Robert Campbell's survey of *The London Tradesman* had noted that the weavers, although 'very ingenious tradesmen', sent to Paris for their designs and thus unwittingly promoted French manufacturers. The point was returned to more forcibly in the 1830s, by which time the London trade had separated out into different branches – from ribbons to furnishing silks. All were accused of producing poor quality work.

If the human consequences of industrial decline were justified from the economists' point of view, to others they were more confusing. The weavers posed a particularly distressing set of questions to the Victorian middle classes, and not just about taxation. Their plight touched on many other things: the new Poor Law, duties and obligations between rich and poor, sanitary measures in towns and the ability of local men to manage local affairs. Above all, the weavers personified the possibility that the new utilitarian frame of mind that had produced the new doctrines of free trade and the new Poor Law might in fact be incompatible with Christian values when pursued too strictly. In February 1853 *The Times* printed a letter from James Trevitt, the vicar of St Philips, one of Bethnal Green's Blomfield churches and located at the Shoreditch end of the parish, near the Old Nichol. He related a recent episode when a grieving and destitute mother had managed to acquire a coffin for her dead child, but had been told brusquely by parish officials that the body could only be buried at the parish's expense if the coffin was opened, the corpse removed and dispatched to a mass grave with no prayers or ceremony. She had no money to pay the cost of a proper funeral. In describing the distress of the woman when she visited him in his home, Trevitt linked the episode explicitly to the authors of the new hard-hearted rationalism. 'I looked, Sir,' he wrote, 'at Adam Smith and Harriet Martineau – they were on the shelf close by – and at Mill who lay on the table, in his two thick volumes; but it was of no use. Malthus himself would have given way.' No doubt to the approval of many readers he chose to break the utilitarian rules and provided a proper Christian burial for the dead infant at no charge to the mother.

FILTH

'The disgusting details which have lately been revealed to that portion of the public who have only heard of Bethnal Green as a low neighbourhood where the weavers live, somewhere in the far east of London, have been the steady growth of recent years.'
The *Illustrated London News*, 24 October 1863.

Newspaper reports of the dreadful conditions in Spitalfields and Bethnal Green had been appearing with increasing regularity since the mid 1820s, and reached a new peak in the 1840s as famine, bad winters, cholera and a notoriously harsh regime on the part of Bethnal Green's work house officials all added to the distress. Misfortune piled upon misfortune and dispatches from the district grew ever more poignant. In 1841 *The Times* reported the 'deplorable state' of Richard Potts and his family, 'a ghostly spectre of the mother and her several children nearly all in a state of nudity.' Potts himself was exhausted and 'past all work but slogging away at a piece of work that will take him three weeks to finish but will only earn ten shillings'. His wife, reported *The Times*, vowed that she would never go to the workhouse because she could not bear to be parted from her children. She 'chose rather to die with them from destitution and starvation'. Charitable effort grew more frantic. In the winter of 1842, the government sent blankets. Balls were organised to raise money for the starving. The City mobilised a distress committee under the patronage of the Lord Mayor and in 1848 the chef Alexis Soyer built a model soup kitchen to provide at least some basic nourishment for the poor. His letter to *The Times* recounts his own visit to the district to see for himself 'that industrious but distressed class of society'. 'We found in many of the houses, five or six in a small room entirely deprived of the common necessaries of life – no food, no fire and hardly any garment to cover their persons, and that during the late severe frost. In one of the attics we visited we inquired of a woman how they subsisted. Her husband, she said, had no employment during the last four moths, and that they merely lived on what the could get by begging in the streets. She added that she and her children had not touched a bit of food for twenty-four hours, the last of which consisted of apples partly decayed and bits of bread given to her husband.'

Bethnal Green's real black decades were the years between 1840 and 1870. Every possible manifestation of urban hell appeared in the district: starvation, freezing winters, ruinous building collapses, overcrowding, untreated sewage, unburied bodies, cholera, blood poisoning, suicide, fever, cruelty, brutality, low pay, unemployment, administrative collapse. A mood of despair often underpins newspaper accounts of these conditions. The local systems that should in theory have helped cope with the distress had failed. There were no solutions. For Soyer, as for many in the 1840s, the weavers' plight represented a cruel conundrum of social geography. 'There are no less than 10,000 poor people in one parish, and hardly any wealthy families among them to give relief.' And yet the weavers and the wealthy elsewhere were directly connected by virtue of the silk cloth 'which has often and even now adorned the persons of thousands of the aristocracy and gentry of their country'.

As the weavers raised questions about the relationship between rich and poor when local solutions failed, so their distress also threw into sharp relief the harsh logic at the heart of the new Poor Law. The system introduced in the 1830s moved parish relief nearer towards the nature of being a penal system. It confined relief to the very destitute, on the theory that a more widespread distribution of 'dole' would act as a dis-incentive to work. It assumed that individual deserving cases would escape the system altogether through being provided for by charitable effort or self-help. Harsh treatment of the non-deserving destitute would act as a deterrent and minimise the cost to local rate payers. The weavers' situation cut across all these assumptions. In today's terms, the twin causes of the weavers' distress were under-employment and low pay, but neither of these concepts really fitted the Poor Law's thinking. It was not that they did not want to work, nor that work was not available. 'I want it to be known,' wrote the crusading vicar of St Phillips to *The Times*, 'that in this district there is plenty of work , but that much of it is so badly paid for (I like their phraseology) that they must slave day and night to live. I want, if it be possible, to put these brave, much enduring, hard-working, right-minded men in a way of living as they ought to live, and as they wish to live – by the fruits of their labour.' As individuals, the weavers had a willingness to work and a desire to help themselves. But as a group their distress was on a scale beyond charitable help and the destitution into which they were so obviously sinking was exactly the process which the Poor Law was in theory supposed to prevent. Society seemed to be playing a particularly cruel trick on the weavers: denying them a means of earning a living and then punishing them further through a system that denied them charitable relief.

The principles of the new Poor Law were also called into question in Bethnal Green by its operation. The local Poor Law Board notoriously ran the most penny-pinching workhouse regime in London. Refusing to give any outdoor relief, officials seemed to place a harsh choice before the destitute weaver: 'take these rules or starve'. Alongside the descriptions of distress in Bethnal Green in the 1840s, *The Times* ran regular accounts of the injustices visited on the heads of the unfortunate inmates of the workhouse by local Poor Law officials. 'There are certain features in the new Poor Law so simply indefensible that only to state them is their severest condemnation,' thundered *The Times* leader following an incident where 15 inmates of the workhouse were sentenced to 21 days hard labour for protesting when officials refused to let them out of the workhouse on Sunday to go to church.

Local administration was also blamed for the filthy state of the district. In 1848 Hector Gavin, a doctor at Charing Cross Hospital, published *Sanitary Ramblings, being sketches and illustrations of Bethnal Green: a type of the condition of the metropolis and other large towns'*. This street by street survey of the parish left no doubt at all about the scandalous conditions in which most Bethnal Greeners lived. Type Street, for example, 'was in the most filthy state possible, the stagnant pools of foetid and putrid mud with their green scum presented an aspect as offensive to the sight as the smell was repulsive: pig stys and dung heaps heightened the foulness of the effluvia'. In Digby Street there was a massive 'table mountain' of manure and a lake of human excrement 'in every stage of offensive and disgusting decomposition'. There were overflowing cess pits, foul privies, pools in which the bodies of dead cats and dogs decomposed, slimy black mud in every street. Gavin also noted houses where fever, measles and whooping cough had already struck and he ended his stomach-churning survey with a more dispassionate look at the mortality statistics for Bethnal Green. The average age of male death in 1841 was 26, as opposed to 32 in Kensington, a parish which had paid more attention to sanitary improvements. Gavin blamed the local authorities in Bethnal Green for allowing such sanitary evils to flourish unchecked in the dwellings of the poor but he concluded that intervention was necessary: 'no hope can possibly be entertained of the necessary charges being effected by the local authorities'. His final conclusion was that the local authorities needed to be helped from above, 'the manner of executing (the necessary works) must be supervised by a central power'.

Accounts of filth continued well into the 1860s. The Old Nichol was the most intensively visited district for evidence of disgusting conditions. But the spotlight fell on Hollybush Place in 1863 thanks to a notorious case of child mortality, attributed to blood poisoning, caused by humans living cheek by jowl with diseased pigs and cows. In Thorold Square in 1863 an *Illustrated London News* correspondent described 'a muddy place with ruinous houses and a rotten, ruined water pump, stuck full of nails which adorns its filthy area'. Entering it from the main street 'the visitor will feel a sickly feeling creep over him and would, if he were previously hungry, discover within himself a sudden loathing for food and a desire for strong drink.' The courts were 'three sides of a miserable little square, like a fetid tank with a bottom of mud or slime'. Inside 'wretched people swarmed from roof to basement along with donkeys, cows, pigs and slaughter houses'. In 1861 John Hollingshead declared that he had known St Phillip's parish in Bethnal Green for 20 years and 'if anything, it seems to me to be getting dirtier and more miserable every year'. Ten years later the Old Nichol Street was as disgusting as ever, according to *The Builder,* then campaigning vigorously for sanitary buildings. The backyards were overflowing with nastiness and the buildings were dangerously near collapse, 'wretched tenements have been doctored to death and they are now bursting asunder in sheer rottenness'. Minerva Street was thick with sodden sludge, heaps of filth and ashes, and choked drains. 'To sum up the general condition of the portion of Bethnal Green district we passed over,' concluded the writer, 'would be to simply say, Bethnal Green is in a most disgraceful and neglectful condition and has been so for many years.'

At the centre of all this was the figure of the weaver, an apparition of foreboding for the mid-Victorian middle classes. However local the breakdown he represented, his plight had national implications, casting a shadow over the fundamental building blocks of social order, including time-honoured work practices. In the 1830s the Bethnal Green Board of Guardians put a stop to the practice of local weavers taking apprentices (for which they were paid a premium), on the grounds that binding a boy to a weaver 'was tantamount to apprenticing the boy to the trade of pauper'. The link between the future of the weavers and the future of the nation was evident to many. 'Can nothing be done to save them and save society?' cried an article about the weavers' plight in *The Builder* in May 1853. 'Let us remember, there is no irremovable reason why these children should grow up to be disorderly and lawless – liars, thieves, perhaps murderers; they were born as capable of good as your own offspring, and with the same nurture and teaching would make useful members of society.' Sanitary reformers called for national intervention to right the wrongs of Bethnal Green, and such calls were echoed from the weavers themselves. 'The Government of my native land ought to interpose their powerful arm to put a stop to such things. Unless they do, civil society with us all is at an end,' said one, at least as reported by Mayhew. In a letter to *The Builder* in June 1853 another summed up their despair. 'I think it would be difficult, if not impossible, in this country to find a body of mechanics forced to toil so incessantly and subsist in such penury as the silk weavers, and what ever will be the end of this state of things (which cannot last much longer) I am at a loss to imagine.'

CRAFTSMANSHIP

'Mrs Stanley Baldwin visited the little colony of silk weavers, descendants of Huguenots, in Cranbrook Street, Bethnal Green, yesterday accompanied by Captain J.H. Bell, the local Conservative candidate. The weavers, who were originally at Spitalfields, wove the velvet for King Edward VII's coronation robes.'

The Times, 9 April 1930.

For the weavers, things were to get worse before they got better. But by the time of Mrs Baldwin's visit to Bethnal Green in 1930, their status had been transformed. Mary Baldwin had come east to pay her respects to Mrs Mary Waite of 45, Cranbrook Street, one of the dwindling number of elderly silk weavers who worked on antiquated hand-looms set up in their upper front rooms. Photographers were present to record the event, and the resulting images of Mrs Baldwin and entourage, crowding over Mrs Waite seated at her spinning wheel, were duly reproduced in several daily newspapers. None of the newspapers gave

Mrs Stanley Baldwin visiting Mrs Waite, 1930.

any reason for the visit, but the presence of the Conservative candidate might have suggested to readers that the visit was less about Mrs Baldwin's womanly interests than her husband's political ambitions. Indeed reports of the visit coincided with accounts of the Conservative leader's new attacks on the Labour government's attachment to the old ideals of free trade. The Friday before, Baldwin had set out his stall as a protectionist in a strong speech to the Primrose League in London. The day of his wife's visit to Bethnal Green, he had travelled to Manchester to speak on the subject of trade and empire at the Free Trade Hall. Here, he directed his appeal to the British workmen who, he argued, enjoyed protection in health, insurance and every other aspect of his working conditions save one: 'but there is no safeguarding against foreign competition of an unfair nature. Why not? That is the most essential fact in the workers' lives. That is the last remnant of *laissez-faire* and it has got to be stripped off quickly'. Readers acquainted with London's industrial past might well have read the reports of Mrs Baldwin's visit and made the connection between the Bethnal Green silk weavers and the British workman's vulnerability to foreign competition of a supposedly unfair nature.

To mid-nineteenth-century London, the silk weavers raised disturbing questions about national progress and Christian values. By the beginning of the twentieth, they had taken on a very different set of associations. By 1900 the only survivors of the trade had retreated to two small colonies in Bethnal Green and now seemed to embody qualities in which the nation could find comfort. The weavers were now presented as standing for continuity, tradition, and the resilience of the honest English workman. Bethnal Green was still poor but no longer a failed state, thanks to the arrival of the London County Council in 1889 which had finally tackled the long-running scandal of the disgusting conditions in the Old Nichol. As one of its first *grands projets* the new council had cleared the disease-infested slums at the top of Brick Lane, replacing them with its showpiece Boundary Street Estate. The arrival in 1901 of a new metropolitan borough had added further impetus to the task of cleaning up Bethnal Green.

By the 1890s, when Jesse Argyle came gathering data for Charles Booth's survey, she found the weavers quietly respectable. They were 'capable and industrious', their alien origins something to admire: they 'still retain the kindly disposition and natural good taste characteristic of the French Huguenot'. This sympathetic portrayal was repeated by a procession of magazine journalists who made the trip east to honour the veteran weavers and wax rhapsodical about their personal qualities. In 1898 the *Daily Graphic* sent a journalist to visit Samuel Higgins, in Gawber Street, and found him a picture of health: 'although 71 years of age he is as active as a young man and his sight is perfect'. There was now no question-mark over the weavers as a group, they were 'long noted as a class for their sprightly, intelligent character'. The Huguenot blood that had once marked their separateness had now become an English pedigree. The weavers were 'so English now that they cannot speak a word of French or even pronounce their names in the French fashion'. This Englishness was, it was noted, in sharp contrast to their Jewish neighbours in Spitalfields. 'The district is still swarming with foreigners, but of a very different stamp from those who in return for a refuge in their misery greatly enriched the country which received them.'

The transformation of the weavers into national living treasures was of course partly to do with their age and rarity. By the time of the 1891 census the numbers employed in silk weaving stood at 4,800, but this was largely accounted for by the Warner factory which was to quit London 4 years later. By the 1920s only a hundred were left and weaving had become a trade entirely undertaken by the elderly, which added to the curiosity value for journalists: 'to see these old people at work is one of the queerest sights in London'. The weavers continued to live and work in their distinctive cottages with large 'long light' warehouse-style windows in the upper floor and spotless interiors: 'you could eat your dinner off the floor of some of the weavers houses', reported one account. The working of the looms was fascinating, and the weavers' poverty was both picturesque and romantic: 'they work not by gaslight but in the soft glow of a lamp. In the centre of the room is a spinning wheel: the light falls on the mellow wood of the looms, polished by the use of hundreds of years'. The humble life, long hours and low earnings were now seen as evidence of moral well-being, and a telling contrast with the feckless next generation. 'The young people won't come to the loom,' said Mr Poynton to H.V. Morton in 1926. 'Its too much like hard work. They won't sit at it from light until dark as we have done all our lives. Young people today want jobs which make it easy for them to go off to the cinema and the dance hall. When we die, there is no one to come after us.'

The age of the elderly weavers reinforced the notion that they personified ancient values of craftsmanship and tradition. This was a easy notion to which to subscribe, as was the parallel notion that these values had somehow been destroyed by the perversions of the industrial revolution which had allowed the Barbarians and Philistines to rampage unchecked across the land. Accounts of the weavers in the early twentieth century are almost always dramatised by some rhetorical passages about past glories before the cheap and shoddy machine age. 'The silent wharf, the empty dock, the broken frame of the old weaver's loom, speak of work and industry well done, well paid, worth doing, pleasurable and pleasure giving,' said Bishop Paget in his essay on East London in the London Society's 1921 volume *London of the Future*. 'It is vain, I suppose, to hope to recapture and win back some of the ancient industries which, like the silk of Spitalfields, gave the place the pride and joy of work done better there than anywhere else; but I own that I should like to see this part of East London famous for something that could hardly be got elsewhere ... hand workmanship (not that generally associated with fancy bazaars) still beats the best that machinery can produce, and the world is coming to understand it.'

The elderly weavers provided living proof that this golden vision of London's craftsman-like past was not imaginary: 'a visit to the weaver colony of London takes one back to the days before the great factory movement was inaugurated and when the science of the engineer had not begun to supplant the skill of the craftsman. For now, as in the past, the workers live and toil in their own little cottages. Many of them have spent upwards of fifty years in the craft – elderly men and women who have dedicated the whole of their waking hours to one of the most intricateof arts. They use the same type of looms, winders and spinning wheels as the Huguenots brought with them, for experience has shown apparently crude devices to be quite as efficient as those gigantic power looms which throb and hum in the weaving sheds of the north'. (There were some ironies in these thoughts. The sort of weaving undertaken in Bethnal Green used the relatively sophisticated semi-mechanised jacquard looms which were as much a product of the industrial revolution as was the fact of the weavers' presence in East London in the first place.)

What had happened to transform Matthew Arnold's pale weaver into the noble and distinguished English craftsman? Two currents in the ebb and flow of the zeitgeist around 1900 seem worth contemplating. On the one hand the weavers received a

Overleaf: The Boundary Street Estate (1895), 1986. Peter Marshall.

benediction from the rise of values associated with the Arts and Crafts movement. On the other, the weavers drew reflected glory from the Crown as a succession of royal occasions underlined the association of silk with royal authority. The deaths of the Duchess of Teck in 1897, the Duke of Teck in 1900 and Queen Victoria in 1901 all provided occasions which called for mourning silk. More important were the two coronations. The purple and crimson velvet for Edward VII's coronation robes was woven by George Dorée, a master weaver from the Cranbrook Street colony in Bethnal Green. For the 1911 coronation Warners supplied most of the brocades for ceremonial use, including the material for the coronation dress itself, and the cloth of gold for the pallium and supertunica, the latter woven at Braintree but by a Bethnal Green-born master craftsman, Albert Parchment. As the name of a pub in Bishopsgate underlined, the Crown and Shuttle went together.

To look first at Arts and Crafts values. The weavers were inevitably caught up in the swelling interest in 'craftsmanship' in the years before the first world war. The word seemed to promise all things to all men. It offered a new narrative for England's past. It humanized the urban proletariat by re-connecting them with their rural counterparts. It offered new nuances to the relationship between rich and poor, casting the merchant or middleman as the villain in the story of social breakdown. To its evangelists it offered magic cures for all ills, guaranteeing personal transformation along with social and educational salvation. Craftsmanship is a particularly interesting concept for London. It was one of the ideas that helped unify the increasingly self-conscious metropolis at the end of the nineteenth century in a positive and flattering way. Craftsmanship had tradition on its side, being clearly connected with the City Livery Companies, which had been managing craft practice and apprenticeships in the City of London since medieval times. In the nineteenth century the Livery Companies underwent something of a modernising revival, moving into a more educational and London-wide role as providers of technical tuition through the City and Guilds Institute, founded in 1878. The Livery Companies' revival reinforced the belief that London was, in Walter Besant's description of East London, 'a city of many crafts' rather than a Babylon created by industrial greed. The appearance of the Victoria County History's volume on Middlesex in 1911 set the historians' seal on the picture of London as a place of specialist skills rather than mass production, workshops rather than factories, and the home of ancient craft traditions. In the Victoria County History's rather idiosyncratic account of London's industries, more space was devoted to book-binding than ship-building. Silk weaving fitted perfectly. It met all the Victoria County History's criteria for an industry that merited a detailed account of its past, namely that the industry had to be long-established in London and have a national importance. Linked as it had been since medieval times to royal protocol and church ritual, silk's place in London's official history was well assured.

During the 1890s the vision of London as a city of many crafts had also appeared in the thinking of the newly formed London County Council (LCC), a body with an obvious interest in promoting a unifying concept for the city. A key figure in the LCC's interest in craftmanship was the civil servant Herbert Llewellynn Smith, a man whose career straddled art, design, social reform and economic policy, all of which bought him into close contact with the East End. Smith had first come to know East London in the 1880s as a resident of Toynbee Hall, where he had helped form the Guild and School of Handicraft, along with the architect C.R. Ashbee. Following the departure of Ashbee and the Guild to Mile End in 1891, Smith had continued to take a benevolent interest in local arts and crafts through the Whitechapel Craft School which moved to Stepney and then in the 1890s to Globe Road in Bethnal Green. Given this background he must have seemed the obvious figure to undertake a survey on the resources for technical education in London, which is what in 1893 the LCC commissioned him to do.

Llewellyn Smith's report reinforced the view that London was naturally suited to small workshops and ill suited to factory production. Smith not only made a virtue out of London's non-factorised character but also identified an over-arching strategic unity by pointing to the historic distribution of trades within London, certain localities being associated with certain trades. This picture of London's economy as an accumulation of craft villages offered the LCC the irresistible opportunity to both respond to local character and provide a centralising focus. Within a few years the Council's Technical Education Board, under the direction of Sidney Webb, had set up a network of local polytechnics and technical institutes with, at the centre, at least for artistic undertakings, the LCC's flagship institution, the Central School of Arts and Crafts, under the directorship of W.R. Lethaby. Plans for a system of local technical museums, each suited to the locality were taken up by C.R. Ashbee, Smith's former colleague at Toynbee Hall, and eventually bore fruit in 1911 with the opening of the Geffrye Museum in Hackney, specifically intended to act as a technical museum for the furniture trade (and thus another comment on the failure of the Bethnal Green Museum to be just that).

So where did the Bethnal Green weavers fit into all this? Did the rise of Arts and Crafts values in local government thinking make any practical difference to the situation of this particular group of skilled craft workers in London? The answer, alas, is no, and although by the 1890s it was probably too late to 'save' the industry in any meaningful way, one cannot help feeling a slight sense of betrayal that Arts and Crafts-minded thinkers did not pay the weavers more attention. But just as the weavers had posed awkward questions for the Utilitarians, so they now posed awkward questions for Arts and Crafts sensibilities. Despite having all the 'good' attributes of hand craftsmanship, they also represented some of the 'bad' attributes of modern industry - long hours, subordination to a capitalist system and an end product that didn't fit aesthetically with Arts and Crafts taste.

The weavers were unfortunate enough to produce work that depended on a high degree of finish and technical complexity. The hand-loom weaving practised in

Bethnal Green since the 1850s was based on the technologically sophisticated jacquard process which activated warp threads by means of punched, cards enabling complex designs to be produced. At its best, this sort of weaving could produce remarkably intricate patterned fabrics made up of 280 threads per inch with lines and decorative effects as fine as any engraving. The patterns tended to be traditional floral patterns harking back to the eighteenth century, which placed them well outside the new Arts and Crafts aesthetic of rough-hewn, hammered 'honesty' to materials. Fifty years earlier the perceived artistic failings of the silk produced in Spitalfields had been used as evidence that the weavers had only themselves to blame for their distress. Something of the same argument resurfaced in the Arts and Crafts era . 'This is shown as an example of skilful weaving, not of fine design' said the author of a 1910 booklet on weaving, illustrating an example of old Spitalfields silk.

If Bethnal Green silk did not sit aesthetically with Arts and Crafts taste, nor did its practice sit with the movement's social beliefs in handicrafts as a liberating force for the free-born Englishman. Broad silk weaving on a Jacquard loom required the weaver to be strapped into a harness, making the machine in effect the master, rather than the tool. This basic fact of production proved a stumbling block for William Morris, the one exception to the lack of interest taken by Arts and Crafts thinkers in the silk weavers. Morris had commissioned weaving firms outside London to produce his designs but in 1877 became intrigued by the process and set up a jacquard silk loom at his own premises in Queens Square, bringing a skilled French weaver to London from Lyons to work it. He later set up an additional four looms at Merton Abbey and did engage a few East London weavers, but the experiment was to prove a dead end. A visitor to the works in 1886 noted Morris's despair at the basic process: 'there was plenty of air and light even in the busiest room, filled with the ceaseless din of whirring looms where the artisans sat bended over their threads, while the lovely play of colours and beauty of texture of the fabrics issuing from under their fingers relieved their work of that character of purely mechanical drudgery which is one of the dreariest features of ordinary factory toil. This was evidently the department that entailed the most arduous and sedentary labour, for as we went out again into the peaceful stillness of the July landscape, Mr Morris reverted with a sigh to the great problem, and asked why men should be imprisoned thus for a lifetime in the midst of such deafening clatter in order to warn a bare subsistence, which the average professional man pockets in comfortable ease.'

Llewellyn Smith also found himself unable to welcome silk weaving into his vision of the future for London's craft industries. His 1893 report for the LCC made a clear distinction between those manufactures that were allied to 'art', and those where the making relied on technological processes and consequently, he assumed, were only a matter of 'manual instruction'. He concluded that 'the artistic crafts should

Spitalfields Study 2, Indian ink on silk 2006. Paddy Killer.

be treated as branches of art rather than technology' but the technologically-based industries should seek their future in science and fit themselves to modern conditions by rooting out bad old trade practices. He placed weaving in the more mechanical group rather than being a 'highly skilled art and handicraft', perhaps a rather unjust categorisation considering that the latter group was deemed to include furniture-making which by the end of the nineteenth century was as mechanised an operation as weaving.

Thus the Bethnal Green silk weavers fell between several stools. Their handicraft was neither simple enough to be fully welcomed into the Arts and Crafts world nor complex enough to evolve into mass production. Their trade appeared to be naturally suited to domestic workshop production, yet this domestic environment was the cause of their economic fragility. Their method of production relied on individual human ingenuity yet it also appeared to enslave the individual. Although the Bethnal Green weavers appeared to fit the simple truths that made the Arts and Crafts movement so appealing on a popular level, they also demonstrated how over-simplistic these Utopian ideas were when applied to the real life situation of London. As the weavers had once challenged the logic of the new Poor Law so they now, in their own small way, demonstrated the real awkwardnesses at the heart of Arts and Crafts philosophy. Was a concentration on expensive hand-made goods, rather than cheap machine-made goods, really the way forward for London's economic prosperity? How could you draw a line between a skilled craftsman working with hand tools and a skilled craftsman working with a machine?

CROWN

'Tis a far cry to the East from Buckingham Palace, still the parish that is notoriously spoken of as 'poor Bethnal Green' has been highly benefited by the marriages of Princess May and the Duchess of York, that is so far as a certain section of the industrious toilers are concerned. The weaving industries have been at work on rich materials for Royalty and the 'gayest Lords and Ladies of the land.'

The *Eastern Argus*, 18 July 1893.

If the hand-loom weavers fell between the art and industry stools for progressive thinkers, there was no such ambiguity for those with a more straightforward view of English society. The weavers reinforced the simple idea of a hierarchical society based on harmonious and mutually enriching links: the weaver made cloth for the King and in return the King protected the weaver. The connection between the highest and the lowest in the land, was the factor that lent the elderly weavers much of their emotional potency in the early years of the twentieth century. And as always, the location of Bethnal Green, right at the heart of the imperial capital, added an extra symbolic charge. In 1893 several newspapers reported a visit by Princess May to Warner's silk mill in Bethnal Green to see the silk being woven for her wedding dress. The visit was described in fairy-tale terms. Albert Parchment was 'the young weaver who worked with his whole soul in the groundwork of shimmering material that was eventually to become the wedding gown of the youthful princess'. But the occasion was even more significant, in the opinion of Frank Warner, the mill's owner: it was no less than 'a turning point in the development of silk manufacture in this country'. There was perhaps something in his claim. The 1891 visit could be said to mark a symbolic turning point in that it reversed the traditional journey whereby the weavers travelled to the palace to petition for help. This time the princess came to the weavers.

Royal patronage was nothing new. The bond between crown and shuttle went back to the medieval period when the wearing of silk was legally confined to those of high birth. Throughout the eighteenth century weavers continued to see royal favour as their main source of protection in times of trouble and by the early nineteenth century the Crown had become publicly involved with the growing distress in the industry. The repeal of the Spitalfields Acts in 1824 began a long catalogue of charitable effort towards the weaver on the part of the Crown. In January 1826 George IV sent £1,000 to the distressed weavers. In February he ordered Windsor Castle to be dressed in English silk. Queen Adelaide endeared herself to the weavers immediately after her accession by ordering silk for a dress in response to a petition written on a fine piece of brocaded ros-de-Naples silk. A meeting of the silk weavers in September 1830 at the Camden's Head in Bethnal Green Road heard Mr Poynton speak of 'Her Majesty's anxiety to benefit the trade of the Spitalfields weavers which he said had caused many persons of distinction to demand home-manufactured silk, and he concluded by observing that he thought Queen Adelaide would be to the Spitalfields weavers what Esther was to the Jews.'

Royal patronage continued under Queen Victoria, who came to the throne in 1838 just as the distress in Spitalfields was entering its most traumatic period. In 1842 the weavers sent an address to Prince Albert urging him to wear English-made silk stockings and in the same year the queen mounted a lavish *bal costumeé* at Buckingham Palace specifically to benefit the weavers. The 2,000 guests were instructed to come in historical costume of any period but made of Spitalfields silk. According to *The Times* this event had created work for 200 looms. By the time of the Great Exhibition English silk was becoming a cause worth supporting for patriotic and philanthropic rather than fashionable reasons. By the last quarter of the century English silk had become the charitable cause of choice in several aristocratic circles, notably through the activities of the Ladies Committee of the Silk Association which had been formed in 1889 by Lady Edgerton of Tatton Park.

The main association aimed to raise the profile of English silk among consumers generally; for example through an exhibition of English silk held at Liberty's in May 1888 and designed to 'bring about the renaissance of this beautiful and once important London industry'. The Ladies Committee, meanwhile, concentrated on their friends. A typical event was held in 1892 at Lady Edgerton's town house in St James' Square. Looms were set up in the drawing room, samples were brought and live weavers demonstrated their skills to her invited guests. These occasions were not entirely private affairs. Many were reported by the newspapers who expressed predictable enthusiasm for this patriotic and imaginative initiative on behalf of the rich to help the hard-pressed poor. There were lots of opportunities to humanise workers and aristocrats alike, representing both as standing side by side in common ground. During the 1893 visit to Warners factory the Princess, it was noted, remembered people's names: 'pointing to a particular loom Her Royal Highness was heard to remark "Why, there's Mr Clark who was weaving those lovely brocades at Lady Edgerton's", pleasing him greatly by saying that she hoped to see him weaving on some future occasion.'

The interest taken by royalty and aristocrats in the Bethnal Green weavers swelled their status before the first world war. If they stood for the virtues of honest craftsmanship, they could also stand for the growing sense of nationhood, stability and continuity under the imperial Crown. Museums reinforced this message. In 1915 the newly formed London Museum acquired several items connected with master-weaver George Dorée, including samples of the velvet woven for the coronation of Edward VII. In the 1920s the museum also acquired a hand-loom and other equipment said to have been used by Mr. Hurable of Spitalfields. The British Museum acquired a piece of silk woven by Alfred Parchment.

The reflected glory of the Crown also enhanced the status of the weavers locally in Bethnal Green. One of the first housing projects undertaken by the newly formed metropolitan borough council was a block of 16 tenements which was named Weavers House and incorporated a plaque reminding inhabitants that the building commemorated the establishment of the ancient craft of silk weaving in this vicinity by fugitives from France. The borough also abandoned plans to demolish the largest remaining colony of weavers' houses around Alma Road to make way for a new borough electricity station. George Dorée, backed by the Weavers Company, argued successfully that the demolition of these cottages, with their distinctive 'long light' upstairs windows would drive out a group of skilled artist-craftsmen. In 1926 the Bethnal Green Museum introduced a permanent exhibition of locally woven silk.

By the 1920s the weavers were embedded into both local and national lore, even despite the receding of Arts and Crafts ideas from progressive thinking. London firms, whether artistic or not, were embracing a factory future in the suburbs. The pioneer craft schools had fled. Ashbee's Guild of Handicrafts established in Mile End in 1891 moved to Chipping Camden in 1901. As the notion of crafts faded from the progressive political landscape so it settled comfortably in the mainstream as something vaguely associated with tradition, national character and moral good. It came into its own in the aftermath of the first world war where crafts provided the perfect solution to the problem of employing disabled service men. The idea of crafts as therapy after trauma also fitted well with the East London weavers. After all, they too were veterans and they too had suffered.

With the death in 1944 of Caroline Coleshill, a spinster of Cranbrook Street who had continued working at her loom well into her seventies, the Bethnal Green weavers finally passed into history. The link they had provided between the wealthy in the west and the workmen in the east continued to echo in the district, thanks to the uniform manufacturer L. Silberston & Sons which took on the role of connecting Bethnal Green with palaces. 'It is remarkable that in the somewhat drab surroundings of Bethnal Green some of the most glamorous uniforms and headdresses of the world are being produced,' said the borough's 1959 guidebook. Dispute about the significance of the weavers also continued to echo. Did they represent the good old days or the bad old days? In the 1950s the two remaining groups of weavers cottages came under threat of demolition. Fifty years earlier the metropolitan borough had abandoned its plan to demolish the Alma Road cottages on the grounds that the buildings housed craftsmen. In the post-war New Jerusalem its mission of utilitarian progress through slum clearances had redoubled in force and the only arguments to be made in favour of preserving the distinctive cottages with their long upstairs windows was sentiment. The debate reached the national papers, who generally were on the side of preservation, *The Times* noting that had the houses been located in Hampstead or Kensington they would become desirable residences. The architectural press noted their 'curiously modern appearances' with the long expanses of glass along the length of the street. To others, however, the weavers cottages represented, not a pre-industrial idyll about which one could get sentimental, but Victorian slums. They were 'the last reminders of the grim past' and should be raised to the ground as soon as possible.

Modern progress prevailed and the streets around Seward Street were demolished to make way for the Dorset Estate, designed by Skinner, Bailey and Lubetkin and completed in 1957 as Bethnal Green's first major slum-clearance scheme. The main group of weavers cottages in Cranbrook Street and Alma Road disappeared under the third of Skinner, Bailey & Lubetkin's Bethnal Green schemes, the Cranbrook Estate, the first stage of which was completed in 1964. As a token link with the past the new estate and its high-rise blocks were named after the streets they replaced. The block Doric House commemorates Doric Road, formerly Alma Road but renamed in 1939 in honour of George Dorée, the poor Bethnal Green weaver who had once woven cloth fit for a King.

4 BETHNAL GREEN AND THE WORKING CLASS

'Bethnal Green is, in this respect, like the nation.'
Michael Young and Peter Willmott, *Family and Kinship in East London,* 1957.

In 1966 *Time* magazine famously stated that every city has its decade and that the 1960s belonged to London. If the same formula was applied to London's boroughs, then Bethnal Green's decade of glory was the 1950s. This was the time when Bethnal Green acquired something close to glamour, when the by-passed borough became a place of pilgrimage for those seeking enlightenment about the lives of ordinary people. Some of the pilgrims put down real roots, most famously Michael Young who founded the Institute of Community Studies from an upstairs room in Victoria Park Square in 1954. Others passed through, bringing their ideas to fruition elsewhere. Peter Benenson, a radical lawyer who later went on to found Amnesty International, moved to Bethnal Green from South Kensington in 1949, spending four years in the borough as an alderman and shaking up the council. Even for those who didn't settle, Bethnal Green became something of a Shangri-La by reputation. Town planners and architects studied its streets, seeking clues to the art and mystery of building communities. In 1953 the place's fame reached Aix-en-Provence when photographs of Bethnal Green street life were presented to the CIAM congress of international architects as signifiers of architecture's new synergy with society. In the visual arts, Bethnal Green's aesthetic of tatty pigeon lofts, decaying brick and scrap metal crept into the world of highbrow art with the conceptual recreation of a Bethnal Green back yard in one of the most influential exhibitions of the decade, *This is Tomorrow*, held in 1956 at the Whitechapel Art Gallery. Shabby old Bethnal Green was so behind the times it had become modern.

Bethnal Green's qualities of modernity were all the more exciting for being hidden. On the surface, the place still looked like a landscape of the past rather than a vision of tomorrow, at least at the beginning of the 1950s. Bombs had left a landscape of dereliction and rubble. The housing was old and dilapidated. Rag-and-bone men still did their rounds on horse-drawn carts. Although Bethnal Green had acquired a tube station in 1946 it was still, to all intents and purposes, a by-passed borough. But to those in the know, it was a place that quickened the pulse with excitement.

Left: 'The Lesson' by Franta Belsky (1958), Lorden Walk 1993. Peter Marshall.

'We were surprised to discover that the wider family, far from having disappeared, was very much alive in the middle of London,' said Michael Young and Peter Willmott in their most famous book *Family and Kinship in East London*, capturing all the elements that made Bethnal Green so special. Bethnal Green was not just any old run-down area, it was a place charged with extraordinary meaning at the heart of the capital.

The main attraction in Bethnal Green during the 1950s was nothing new. The one thing for which the district had long been famous was its proletarian population. As the parish had once been synonymous with weavers, so now the borough stood for the working class, its role in this respect completely confirmed by statistics. In the 1930s the *New Survey of Life and Labour* had estimated that 91% of the borough's families were working-class. By the 1950s nothing had changed. 'Most of the 54,000 people it contained in 1955 belonged to the "working class",' stated Young and Willmott firmly. What had changed between the 1930s and 1950s was the national mood and the alteration was very much in Bethnal Green's favour. Empathy and sentiment had given way to respect, indeed admiration, for 'the common people' and the way they lived their lives.

As in so much else, war was the catalyst of change. In his 1947 essay on *The English People* George Orwell had even suggested a precise point when class-relations turned towards a new direction. 'During the bad period of 1940 it became clear that in Britain national solidarity is stronger than class antagonism.' Orwell's essay went on to warn against slipping back into the old ways of 'class feeling'. Despite winning the war Britain had to learn afresh what sort of country it was, look at itself more honestly and recognize a more truthful sense of self. 'The real England is not the England of the guide-books,' he told his readers. 'Blackpool is more typical than Ascot, the top hat is a moth-eaten rarity, the language of the BBC is barely intelligible to the masses.' Orwell was not over romantic in his generalisations about 'the English people proper, the working masses' but he had no doubts that the country's destiny was in their hands and that greater social equality rather than greater liberty was the correct national goal.

If war was the point at which the previously separate classes decided to come together in marriage, then the post-war period was the honeymoon. Romance was still in the air but the heat of passion had cooled and this was the time for each party to get to know the other a little better. Bethnal Green's significance in the process of getting to know 'the English people proper' is of course largely assured by Michael Young's Institute of Community Studies (ICS), established in 1954 with the express aim of informing the state about their citizens. As Young and Willmott explained a few years later, 'the Institute was based on the assumption that policy makers and administrators were (to use a somewhat elusive term) insufficiently aware of the needs or views of the working-class people who form the bulk of the users of social services'. The explicit aim of the Institute was to 'conduct research which would have a bearing on policy' but it also wished its work to be readable by a lay market, which indeed it succeeded in doing. The Institute's corpus of work, sometimes known as 'the Bethnal Green Studies', is famous for its literary qualities. Its most celebrated book, *Family and Kinship in East London,* is a much-lauded text, still in print and often described as a 'classic of modern sociology'.

The ICS was not alone in feeling at home in Bethnal Green. Other observers were drawn to the borough. The attraction was partly the infrastructure of support for academic research provided by University House, an institution which had begun life as a club for unskilled men organised by Oxford House. By the 1950s University House had developed a life of its own as a centre for legal advice, social research and voluntary activity under the direction of its warden J.L. Peterson. Many important Bethnal Green initiatives sprang from University House, notably the borough's council of social services, founded in 1953 as a pioneering attempt to coordinate all local voluntary organisations. University House made social research in post-war Bethnal Green possible. What made it desirable was the borough's reputation as a uniquely interesting place. As discussed below, immediately after the war Bethnal Green was discovered to be a model village, the ideal working-class community. The timing of this discovery was no accident. It is irresistible to read into the intelligentsia's enthusiasm for Bethnal Green in the late 1940s the larger story of Britain's aspirations for itself after the war. In Bethnal Green the academics saw a group of people who appeared to have flourished despite, and perhaps because of, isolation; who had undergone a common experience of suffering, who lived modestly, with warm good humour and who thrived on equality of status. Bethnal Green was indeed like the nation.

Victory Café, Hackney Road, 1986. Peter Marshall.

VILLAGE

*'The village community is associated in people's minds with rural organisation. A
community like social group sometimes survives or grows, however, in the midst of a
conurbation. Bethnal Green is such a place. It is not surprising therefore that it should
have attracted many students to its study. It has a rarity value. At least we think it does.'*
Ronald Frankenberg, *Communities in Britain*, 1966.

The discovery of special qualities in Bethnal Green can be traced back to a report
produced in February 1946 by Ruth Glass and Maureen Frankel for the Association
for Planning and Regional Reconstruction. Originally produced as a cheap
typewritten pamphlet, 'A Profile of Bethnal Green' entered the wider public
domain when an illustrated version appeared in the second issue of *Contact* books.
Here, it was entitled 'How they live at Bethnal Green' and was presented with all
the visual glamour that made *Contact* such an seductive read for the post-war
intelligentsia. The graphic style was adventurously modern, using different
typefaces, coloured paper and a jazzy layout. The illustrations included a Victorian-
flavoured montage by *Contact*'s art editor F.H.K. Henrion and a photo-essay by
Erich Auerbach, showing black and white, social documentary-style images of old
women in pubs and urchins on bomb-sites. The aestheticised visual presentation
was not the only thing that marked the article as a new way of looking at the old
East End. Glass and Frankel's analysis of Bethnal Green was a masterly re-branding
of the district, turning its perceived failings into strengths. They presented the
borough not as evidence of the mistakes of the past but as a blue print for the New
Jerusalem of the future. 'The outstanding feature of present-day Bethnal Green is
that, however aged, poor and shabby, it has solved one of the urgent problems of
modern planning, how to create an urban community, the component parts of
which are clearly distinct and yet integrated into a coherent whole.' Bethnal Green
was no longer a place to be pitied but a place from which to learn.

Glass and Frankel's account was no sentimental rhapsody. It was a serious analysis,
which left no doubt that physical reconstruction and economic revitalisation were
urgent needs for the bomb-damaged and shabby East End district. Their main point
was to argue that this reconstruction should not sweep away the old wholesale. It
should acknowledge and preserve both the existing neighbourhoods and the
'positive social relationships' which flourished therein. The argument was given a
slightly sentimental cast by the notion that Bethnal Green could be thought of as a
village. Glass and Frankel emphasised the borough's 'village characteristics' of being
physically compact and self-contained. The behaviour of the people conformed to
the popular stereotype of village life: neighbourliness was the norm, people met
out of doors in the borough's open spaces – here likened to village greens – or in
the back streets and courtyards, where 'every summer evening the chairs are put out
on the pavement; the women sit chatting until bed time while fathers and

grandfathers sit on their doorsteps reading their papers and smoking their pipes. You will see such pictures of friendliness and sociability everywhere in the Borough.'

Villages also appeared in the vision of reconstruction presented by Patrick Abercrombie in his *County of London Plan* published in 1943. In Abercrombie's rather patrician thinking, London's various districts were all 'descended from ancient villages' and one of the issues of reconstruction was to 'disengage' them from the force-fields that had pulled them into the anonymous metropolis and submerged them beneath an aesthetically unattractive veneer of traffic, unplanned industry and 'large areas of dreary and monotonous streets'. Abercrombie's plan envisaged a shining new East End reconfigured virtually from scratch as a series of village islands, each small, clean and surrounded by its own protective girdle of green space. Where his villages differed from Glass and Frenkel's was that his creations erased all trace of their Victorian past. The new Utopian Bethnal Green was illustrated in figure 17 of Abercrombie's plan as virtually a new town with white modern buildings and tree-lined boulevards, dividing up the space in new ways and leaving only the Museum, churches and the existing patches of green space as physical reminders of what had gone before. By contrast, Glass and Frenkel's vision warned against throwing out the baby of social harmony along with the bath-water of old buildings. 'In grouping these new homes the present neighbourhood pattern will have to be carefully observed.'

Glass and Frenkel's presentation of Bethnal Green as a place which had something important to teach the outside world about social well-being was novel, to say the least. The two academics argued their case by identifying two of the borough's basic characteristics as fundamental to its social cohesion. Firstly, everyone had the same status. Although 'subtle distinctions' existed between people and streets, these were 'but a fraction of the gap that separates Bethnal Green from Bayswater'. Glass and Frenkel accorded great importance to shared status as a factor in communal loyalty '... existing social differences are not broad enough to disturb Bethnal Green's essential homogeneity. Everybody is poor and hence competition does not spoil personal relationships. ' "We are not higher than anyone else; we are all on the same level and so we all get on together," one Bethnal Green housewife told us. This fact was even more important in creating people's loyalty to the Borough than all the other characteristics which have been described.'

The second ingredient of social harmony was the borough's cultural self-sufficiency which the academics saw as flourishing despite, rather than because of, interference from outsiders. Dismissing the nineteenth-century settlement movement as misplaced effort ('Oxford dons ... aiming to become 'the Squires of the East End'), Glass and Frenkel saw the working-class monoculture as well able to look after itself. 'Many (settlers) discovered when they had got to know the people, that, while everyday necessities were sorely needed, moral support was hardly required, for

Bethnal Green is a place where neighbours can rely upon each other, where there is a general atmosphere of friendliness, of strength and independence The people do not apologise for their surroundings. They are proud of Bethnal Green and intensely loyal to their community.'

This all added up to a new analysis. The social homogeneity and self-sufficient isolation that Glass and Frankel so admired were precisely the aspects of the borough that had been identified as its main problems before the war. If Frankel and Glass's reading ushered in a new orthodoxy about Bethnal Green, the old orthodoxy held that isolation and class-homogeneity were matters for alarm rather than admiration. For at least one other observer in the 1940s, the old orthodoxy still rang true. P.J.O Self saw in Bethnal Green a monoculture that remained leadenly unleavened. 'Bethnal Green contains no diversity of classes such that the educated and the rich can contribute in their several ways to the welfare of the community. There is only a working class; once very poor, still poor; once the victim of circumstances and so without initiative, still limited and handicapped in all directions, and partly because of the past, unequal to using what power it has.' To Self, the people were very far from self-sufficient, however warm and friendly. 'The people have still not the resources, either of wealth or brains fully to be masters of their fate.'

Self was not alone in subscribing to the old ways of thinking. Another piece of received wisdom about Bethnal Green was that its homogeneous population was a stagnant one. Robert Sinclair's 1956 book *East London* provided a typical expression of this view, which identified Bethnal Green as particularly unhealthy because its families tended to stay put. 'And a family which has spent three lifetimes in a Bethnal Green street will remain in poverty for eternity unless it dies out or is forcibly moved into another way of life. Such stagnant pools of humanity influence the pattern of the complex currents of the long drawn out revolution of East London. Their presence provides the backward eddies; yet the time comes when a solid cake of people will break up, like the logs freed from a dam and will alter the pattern of the stream again.' The imagery of the 'stagnant pool of humanity' has a turn-of-the-century ring to it and Sinclair's views, more fully expounded in his 1937 polemic *Metropolitan Man,* reflected the debate about urban degeneracy that had ebbed and flowed around public opinion since the 1890s. Bethnal Green's place in this debate can be traced back to a chapter in the first series of Booth's *Life and Labour*. Here, Hubert Llewellyn Smith had advanced a startling hypothesis linking urban poverty with low rates of immigration into London from rural areas. Comparing data from Booth's survey with census data about place of birth, he concluded that London's population drew its vigour from the influx of healthy country folk. 'London is to a great extent nourished by the literal consumption of bone and sinew from the country.' Where this sustaining stream of new blood dried up, second-generation Londoners fell into a cycle of physical and mental degradation. 'Why is there so little local life and sentiment in

East London,' asked Llewellyn Smith. 'Why is it hardly possible to conceive an excited throng crying "Well played Bethnal Green!" with the same spirit which nerves the men of Bradford to crowd enthusiastically to the football field on a cold and drizzling November afternoon?' Bethnal Green was the main proof of his thesis by being one of London's poorest districts and at the same time 'the most purely London district', the area where 87% of the population was London-born. It contained the Old Nichol, 'the absolute low-water mark of immigration for the whole of London'. 'We may cry London for the English if we will,' declaimed Llewellyn Smith. 'He would be rash indeed who cried London for the Londoner.'

Although Llewellyn Smith's logic was challenged at the time his theory appeared, the vague notion that the East End in general and Bethnal Green in particular was a stagnant pond where the unfittest people festered proved difficult to shift. Statistics confirmed that Bethnal Green continued to be demographically insular. By 1911 the percentage of London-born inhabitants had fallen to 84.8% but by 1921 it was back up again to 87.1%. It was not until the 1950s that the equation of low migration with unhealthiness and degeneracy was finally put to rest. Although Glass and Frankel paved the way, it was really Young and Willmott in *Family and Kinship* who killed it off by introducing the new notion that low migration was in fact the sign of a healthy population. Demographic insularity, they suggested, should be read positively as indicating strong kinship links, stability and an enviable sense of community and continuity. The fact that in the 1951 census 'Bethnal Green had a higher proportion of residents born in it than did almost any other London borough' was a thoroughly good thing. What had looked like a brackish pond was in fact a village all along.

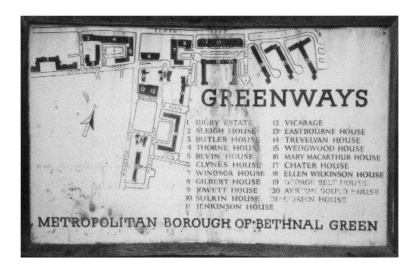

Greenways Estate plan, 2005.

HOUSING

'And she brought me face to face with the endless argument about Bethnal Green in which normally unemotional words like dog, rabbit-hutch, backyard and parlour are ranged against phrases like "sea of asphalt", " inhuman scale", " sanitary desert" and so on. The new prefabs are simply the latest temporary exhibit in what is not only a sociologist's zoo, but an architectural museum. It is all there, every mean or patronising or sentimental or brutal or humane assumption about the housing needs of the urban working class.'

Colin Ward, BBC radio talk, December 1962.

One of the most insistent refrains in Glass and Frankel's article is the notion that Bethnal Green had its cake and ate it in terms of accommodating difference within unity. They detected this quality in the borough's personal relationships, and in its physical appearance. 'Although at first all the houses and streets look very much alike to you, you will discover a good deal of variety. For there is both unity and differential.' The people, according to the two academics, had internalised two overlapping strands of community loyalty: firstly to the borough itself and then to the local neighbourhood. They indentified five clearly-demarcated neighbourhoods in Bethnal Green, all harmoniously integrated into a larger whole, even 'the major foreign colony' around Brick Lane where 'English, Eastern European and Portuguese Jews live side by side with Polish and Lithuanian Catholics'. Both strands of loyalty contributed to 'the social cohesion which is such a striking feature of Bethnal Green'. Preserving both, they argued, was key to reconstruction: 'the sense of belonging to the individual streets and groups should not disturb but be part of the sense of belonging to the larger unit; it will now be the planner's job to preserve the combination of diversity and unity while proceeding with the thorough reconstruction which has long been overdue'.

Glass and Frankel provided no real directions as to how this might be accomplished beyond a gnomic warning that contradictions lay ahead: the divisions of the old neighbourhoods must be carefully studied but should 'neither be obliterated nor over-emphasised'. By the latter they meant the creation of small neighbourhood units that were so self-contained as to lose touch with the larger whole, as for example might be the case with the 'foreign colony' where it was obviously undesirable to turn it into a ghetto. Equally difficult to reconcile was the notion that Bethnal Green was already socially harmonious and yet still in need of reconstruction. How much of the existing fabric should be preserved: how much destroyed? Did the existing social harmony depend on the existing physical layout of the houses and streets? What was the balance to be struck between demolishing the old housing stock, in the name of slum clearances, and preserving the old housing stock, in the name of respecting existing family networks?

These were precisely the questions to which Young and Willmott returned in *Family and Kinship*. The area of policy to which they intended their study to

The Dorset Estate, 1993. Peter Marshall.

The Cranbrook Estate, 1993. Peter Marshall.

contribute was housing and their book argued for privileging the personal networks that already existed, even if this meant preserving the old housing stock. The evidence for the prosecution was the Essex housing estates to which East Enders had been moving *en masse* since the 1920s. Young and Willmott argued that what might have been gained in housing standards had been lost in social cohesion. The new estates, in Young and Willmott's view, lacked the two essential components of a sustainable community: a settled population and kinship networks. 'Either length of residence or localised kinship does something to create a network of local attachments, but when they are combined, as they are in Bethnal Green, they constitute a much more powerful force than when one exists without the other.' Young and Willmott painted two contrasting pictures of social well-being: 'Bethnal Greeners are not lonely people: whenever they go for a walk in the street, for a drink in the pub or for a row on the lake in Victoria Park, they know the faces in the crowd.' By contrast, 'that busy social life is now a memory' for the unfortunates who had moved to the Essex estate of 'Greenleigh' (a thinly disguised Debden). 'Shopping in the mornings amid the chromium tiles of the Parade is a lonely business compared with the familiar faces and sights of the old street market.' In a later publication Young and Willmott compared Bethnal Green with the middle-class suburb of Woodford. The place came out slightly better than Greenleigh in terms of friendliness but Young and Willmott read Woodford's 'friendliness' in rather a snide way as bound up with middle-class snobbishness. This later study added further definition to the picture of Bethnal Green as a place of warm humanity whose existing housing stock, shabby though it might be, was part of the place's eco-system.

The target of Young and Willmott's argument was not just the received wisdom of decanting people out of the crowded inner cities. They also questioned the massive slum clearance schemes then beginning to wrench Britain's inner-city landscapes into new shapes. 'The physical size of reconstruction is so great that the authorities have been understandably intent upon bricks and mortar... Yet even when the town planners have set themselves to create communities anew as well as houses, they have still put their faith in buildings, sometimes speaking as if all that was necessary for neighbourliness was a neighbourhood unit, for community spirit a community centre. If this was so, then there would be no harm in shifting people about the country, for what is lost could soon be regained by skilful architecture and design. But there is surely more to a community than that. The sense of loyalty to each other amongst the inhabitants of a place like Bethnal Green is not due to buildings. It is due far more to ties of kinship and friendship which connect the *people* of one household to the *people* of another.' Young and Willmott concluded their book with a plea for housing policies which flowed from existing social groups and their preferences, even if putting this into practice meant slaying some of planning's sacred cows. 'It would mean sacrificing some of the many projected open spaces earmarked in the plans for future public gardens... It would certainly mean saving as many as possible of the existing houses, where these are structurally sound, by installing within the old fabric new bathrooms, lavatories and kitchens.' Where existing houses were beyond recovery, it would also mean 'moving as a block the social groups, above all the wider families, to which people wish to belong'. Moving street and kinship groupings as a whole, in Young and Willmott's view, would allow reconstruction to proceed 'without squandering the fruits of social cohesion'.

The core of the research for *Family and Kinship* was carried out in 1953–55 and by the time the book came out in 1957 its argument had been overtaken by events. The ideas about community 'discovered' in Bethnal Green were already being returned to the area but not in a form of which Young and Willmott approved. The tower blocks were beginning to rise and acres of old terrace houses had already been designated as unfit for human habitation. New housing in post-war Bethnal Green came from two sources: the London County Council, which had powers to build in all areas of London, and the metropolitan borough itself. Between the two of them, they built about 8,000 new homes in Bethnal Green between 1950 and 1980, of which about half came from the local council – a surprisingly high proportion given the borough's small size. Bethnal Green's housing drive began in the early 1950s with a change of mood and ambition. The council had long been Labour-controlled but tended to be cautious, at least according to P.J.O. Self in 1945, 'the solid Labour majority on the borough council is more a reflection of the "Doubting Thomas" attitude than a resolve to transform society'. Around 1950 a wind of change blew into the housing committee, which has been attributed to the arrival of Peter Benenson as the new chairman. The borough acquired a bullish new vision for its housing, and launched two five-year housing plans in 1951 and 1954, both intending to rival the LCC in their scale. It embarked on the largest slum-clearance scheme undertaken by any metropolitan borough after the war, and brought in some top architectural firms of the day to realise its vision in a thoroughly modernist way.

It is inconceivable that Benenson and his fellow housing-committee members did not subscribe to the Glass and Frankel view of Bethnal Green as a model community based on separate neighbourhoods and accommodating difference within overall unity. The new modern housing estates speak eloquently of Glass and Frankel's instructions that local divisions should neither be obliterated nor over-emphasised. All the borough's new estates were broadly modernist in style, but with considerable variety in form and finish – sometimes thanks to the intervention of the council, as for example in the Cranbrook Estate where the council insisted, against the wishes of the architect, that the facings should be brick rather than concrete. Overall Bethnal Green modernised its look, but each neighbourhood acquired a distinctive architecture of its own, although the effect was rather diluted by the LCC which sprinkled its standard slab-blocks all over the borough.

Bethnal Green council employed three architectural firms for most of its housing projects: Skinner, Bailey & Lubetkin; Denys Lasdun; Yorke Rosenburg & Mardell, all three associated with thoughtful approaches to public housing. The first large-scale commission in the borough was a slum-clearance scheme south of Hackney Road providing new homes for the 250 families who had been living there in streets of run-down weavers cottages. Skinner, Bailey & Lubetkin received the commission and devised a scheme based on 11-storey Y-shaped blocks, the same structure that the firm had previously used in Finsbury and which, according to D.C. Bailey, offered 'a combination of economic planning with good aspect, light and privacy'. Design was bespoke: the elevations were faced in stone with a pattern of staggered windows which were supposed to reflect the internal divisions and introduce movement and vitality into the façades. A library was built alongside the housing blocks and the new estate was named the Dorset Estate, in honour of the Tolpuddle martyrs, who also supplied the names for the individual housing blocks.

More experimental in terms of architectural form were Denys Lasdun's two variations on the 'cluster block'. Lasdun's first designs in Bethnal Green were two small eight-storey blocks on a butterfly plan, completed in 1958 on a cleared bomb-site, south of Roman Road. Trevelyan House and Sulkin House had a somewhat Bethnal Green-like air to them, looking faintly like ramshackle cottages stacked up on top of one another. These experiments were followed by a more ambitious scheme for a slum-clearance site south of Hackney Road. Here, Lasdun produced Keeling House, a 16-storey block of maisonettes and flats stacked up in a tripartite 'vertical street'. By the time Keeling House appeared the old buzzwords of community and neighbourhood had been superceded in the architectural world by a new set of vocabularies and concepts. Buildings had to demonstrate 'grain', meaning the feel of the urban environment; and 'cluster', a quality which recognised the need to balance privacy and communality. Lasdun's block had both cluster and grain in theory, but did it succeed? 'I could not decide on the strength of a casual visit,' mused Colin Ward, in 1963, 'whether Mr Lasdun's experiment was a dark fortress or a vertical street. He hoped, by bringing the short wings of the block (which cluster round a central core containing lifts and services), within talking distance of each other to reduce the isolation which many tenants of the new flats complain of. A survey by Willmott and Cooney suggests that he had not really succeeded in this aim but at least he hasn't pursued it at the expense of anyone's privacy.'

'Willmott and Cooney' referred to two Institute of Community Studies researchers, Peter Willmott and Edmund Cooney. The ICS was of course very much in favour of re-housing people within their old neighbourhoods but very much against putting them in tall blocks, on the grounds that people disliked them. 'The research we did at our Institute from 1953,' wrote Michael Young in 1980, 'showed that hardly

Keeling House, 1993. Peter Marshall.

anyone living there liked high-rise blocks or large estates; we appealed, in vain at that time, to architects and planners not to go on doing what they wanted rather than what ordinary people wanted. Neither a book, nor a whole library of books, could make the plea forcibly enough; not until Ronan Point did opinion finally crystallise against high-rise blocks.'

To Michael Young and his colleagues, the borough council's belief that community spirit would continue to flourish when people were transplanted to clean, new high-rise flats was at best a leap in the dark and at worst positively destructive to the sense of place on which community spirit depended. They quoted with approval one local woman: 'I suppose the buildings in Bethnal Green aren't all that good but we don't look on this as a pile of stones. It isn't the buildings that matter. We like the people here.' In Young and Willmott's vision, terrace houses were not potential slums but sacred spaces where the soul of Bethnal Green resided. These were cottage-homes where people lived modestly in harmony with the natural world. In one of the most famous passages from *Family and Kinship* they root the Bethnal Greeners deeply to their patches of land. 'Many of the yards are packed with clothes hanging on the line, prams, sheds, boxes of geraniums and pansies, hutches for rabbits and guinea pigs, lofts for pigeons and pens for fowls... Dilapidated but cosy, damp and friendly, in the eyes of most Bethnal Greeners these cottages *are* the place.'

Needless to say, such views easily attracted criticism at the time. The hardline modernists saw the repudiation of architecture as a tool in social engineering as the ultimate in reactionary sins. Fellow sociologists accused them of sentimentalising poverty, romanticising the working-class 'Mum', and displaying a snobbish disapproval of those who rejected the class *mores* they were born into by 'bettering themselves' and moving out to suburbia. The idiosyncratic methodology even came in for attack, 'the poor sociologist's substitute for a novel' said some. Later in life Michael Young conceded that his critics might have had a point. In 2001 a newspaper interview quoted him as saying 'wistfully' of his time in Bethnal Green, 'Yes, I probably was guilty of romanticising the working classes; I didn't realise how narrow-minded they could be.' But in the context of the 1950s, a romantic and sentimental approach to the task of bringing the working classes officially into the fold of 'us' rather than 'them' was perhaps no bad thing. And looking back from the twenty-first century, the arguments for preserving existing housing stock seem more reasonable than they evidently appeared at the time. Young's aim for his research was that it should inform and influence official policy. Housing might be counted as one of its short-term failures. Had the *Family and Kinship* point of view prevailed, less of Bethnal Green's unique streets of weavers' 'long-light' cottages might not have been lost.

The architects whose names are missing from the roll call of those who built in 1950s Bethnal Green are Alison and Peter Smithson. It is in some ways a fortunate omission for the borough since their 'New Brutalist' style is an acquired taste, even in architectural circles. But they would have been an appropriate choice given the degree to which their work drew intellectual inspiration from the Bethnal Green street. The Smithsons were the channel through which Bethnal Green moved into the glamorous world of modernist architectural theory. In the 1953 CIAM architectural congress at Aix-en-Provence it was the Smithsons who presented photographs of Bethnal Green's landscape juxtaposed with the architects' own esoteric diagrams and designs, collaged to incorporate the figures of Marilyn Monroe and a selection of international film stars and philosophers. It was an irresistable bricolage of the real, the glamorous and the intellectual. The photographs were the work of their friend Nigel Henderson, who lived in Bethnal Green in the late 1940s. It was through visiting Henderson that the Smithsons encountered 'the East End street', the idea of which appeared in their architectural theorising as a signifier of the spontaneity and vitality to which architecture should aspire. Further thoughts about movement, identity and association led to some over-wrought ideas about housing which eventually found physical expression in the East End courtesy of the Greater London Council, who built Smithson's monolithic caterpillar block of Robin Hood Gardens in Poplar in 1967. This attempt to create a street in the sky has not survived well and today it is difficult to see how its pedestrian interpretation of 'the street' has anything at all to say about spontaneity, vitality or community.

OUTSIDERS

'Jews are the only people now who have large families – no one else can afford it. Soon they will outnumber us. They own all the shops and factories – only one shop in twenty in the main street of Bethnal Green is owned by a non-Jew. Related how he and his friends, when schoolboys, had made a practice of stoning Jewish boys as they came out of school'.

James Robb, reporting an interview with a 58 year old Bethnal Green man, 1954.

One of the criticisms made of *Family and Kinship* is that its rosy picture contains no hint that such a warm and well-balanced community might harbour anti-social forces. There are no delinquent teenagers, no violent fathers and no evidence of racism or prejudice towards those who were outside the family and kinship networks. Long settlement and extended families created a community that was 'not easily penetrated by external influences' said Young and Willmott proudly in their 1960 book comparing Bethnal Green with Woodford. 'Just because it is internally so cohesive the local community is able to erect a wall against disturbing ideas from outside.' This, they judged a good thing because it inoculated Bethnal Greeners against the contamination of 'putting on airs' and other middle-class pretensions. But of course cultural walls had a dark side. What Young and Willmott did not address was the question of how Bethnal Green coped with outsiders.

Young and Willmott were not the only observers of Bethnal Green during the 1940s and 1950s. Others drew different conclusions from the borough. P.J.O Self's account of voluntary organisations in Bethnal Green has already been mentioned. His survey was primarily concerned with the future of social services in the borough but from this perspective he believed that 'the ideal of a self-sufficient Bethnal Green looks well into the future'. This was, he judged, partly because the existing largely voluntary services were not yet sufficiently strong to develop genuine mechanisms of local control, but also because of the prevailing culture. Like Glass and Frankel he recognised a fierce sense of local loyalty but interpreted this less as evidence of a natural spirit of collectivism as a by-product of individualism, which he saw as the basic characteristic of the Bethnal Greeners. They were, in his view, 'individualists by nature and circumstances'. He was also considerably less complimentary than Glass had been about their ability to exercise political power, 'the people have no real faith in their own power to effect changes and – partly a cause, partly a result – small initiative to learn anything. Their way of life is unimaginative.' Consequently, Self saw the activities of external bodies, such as the settlements and other social services, as critical to the borough's collective well-being. '(The settlements) are ceasing to be foreigners and are becoming rooted in the borough's life. They are no longer so much helping those who cannot help themselves as providing a framework within which people can use their own initiative.'

Self's view of the Bethnal Greeners as passive individualists harked back to earlier observations. In the 1920s, Constance Harris had arrived in the borough to investigate the way the Bethnal Greeners used their leisure time and had emerged with somewhat depressing conclusions. She painted a picture of a culture which accepted things as they are. 'The majority of them are satisfied with plenty to eat and drink, many and cheap clothes the same as everybody else buys and as little work for as much money as possible.' She saw a lack of sustained effort and a high incidence of anti-social individualism, which she attributed to child-rearing. 'The East End child is given his freedom far too soon, with the result that he is an ardent individualist, failing to realise his responsibilities.'

Childhood experience was also a factor in another post-war study of the Bethnal Greeners. This was carried out in 1947-9 by James Robb as part of Ph.D research at the London School of Economics. Robb, a psychologist from New Zealand, was interested in how national character might be explored through psychoanalytic techniques. The hypothesis that brought him to Bethnal Green was his hunch that generalisations about national character paid insufficient attention to variations between social classes. In order to explore this he needed a one-class district and Bethnal Green was of course very well suited, particularly as the class that most interested him was the working class. Bethnal Green was even more appropriate to his research in that he wanted to look specifically at ethnic or race prejudice and Bethnal Green had a reputation as one of London's most anti-Semitic areas. In the 1937 municipal elections, the British Union of Fascists polled a higher proportion of votes in Bethnal Green than in any other part of Britain. Robb's work was published in 1954 under the title *Working-Class Anti-Semite*.

Bethnal Green had not been immediately affected by the mass migrations of Russian Jews in the late nineteenth century. Jewish immigration into the East End had initially been concentrated in Stepney, Aldgate and Spitalfields, all districts with existing Jewish presences. In 1881 there were 921 people of foreign birth in Bethnal Green, as compared to 16,000 in Stepney. As the community settled, so the people spread. In 1901 Bethnal Green's Jewish population had risen to 3.5%, mostly living in the new Boundary Street Estate. By the 1920s Jewish families accounted for around 12% of the borough's population. By the 1930s the sense of tribal difference between Jews, Irish and English was part of Bethnal Green's cultural landscape, as it was throughout the East End, sometimes spilling over into violence, particularly when stirred up by fascists. Bethnal Green, the insular and poor borough, became prime recruiting ground for the British Union of Fascists during the 1930s and the party made their local headquarters in Green Street.

By the time Robb came to Bethnal Green, awareness of the Holocaust had caused anti-Semitism to disappear from public discourse; but Robb, like many, believed it survived in hearts and minds of individuals. Robb was concerned with individual psychology, but he linked this absolutely to group values and behaviour: 'it is clear that because of his different background and experience the Bethnal Green man will interpret many facts in a way that will not be immediately obvious to the outsider'. Exploring this further, his book included a chapter on 'some aspects of life in Bethnal Green' and a sophisticated analysis of the social circumstances that might predispose the area to produce a high proportion of prejudiced personalities. Robb's analysis makes a fascinating comparison to *Family and Kinship*. Like Young and Willmott he saw low social mobility, high-density living and a warm mother-baby relationship as key to explaining the typical Bethnal Green personality but he drew different conclusions. To Robb, although Bethnal Greeners start life with the security of a particularly warm relationship with their mother, this disappears very early on in the child's life as it is 'forced out' into the adult world of the street to seek alternative comfort in unisex gangs. Here, group solidarity is closely related to 'very marked aggressiveness which is displayed in almost any circumstances, and is nearly always masked by a display of joviality'. The combined effect of mother and gangs left Bethnal Green men, according to Robb, with a precariously fragile personality and a predisposition to anxieties that could easily turn to psychosis.

Robb was careful to point out that his findings did not suggest that child-rearing in Bethnal Green automatically led to antisocial behaviour. His research included a group of tolerant Bethnal Green men who proved to his satisfaction that 'if all goes well', anxieties could be accommodated. However for some, 'a predisposition to open hostility towards out-groups is formed when early childhood and later social experiences combine to produce an expectation of affection and security insufficient to meet the needs of the personality'. The Jews of Bethnal Green were unfortunate enough to fulfill all the characteristics of a scapegoat group and 'it is not surprising that, when a man of Bethnal Green seeks an out-group towards which his aggressive impulses are to be turned, he should chose his Jewish neighbours'.

Bethnal Green's Jewish population had always posed something of a problem to received wisdom about the area. For the stagnant-pool school of thought, anything that diluted the lumpen proletariat was in theory a good thing. However, the Jewish presence was invariably presented as concentrating rather than diluting the problem. The division between Jew and Gentile was seen as so impenetrable as to render impossible any improvement of one by the other. In the 1890s Llewellyn Smith had decided that the Jewish population was subject to a completely separate kind of population movement. Jewish immigration came from abroad, rather than the country, and therefore different rules applied: 'whereas English London is kept up in bone and sinew and energy by the country element pouring in from above… Jewish London is kept down by the foreign element drifting in from below'. Llewellyn Smith saw the only effect of one on the other as competition for space, as upwardly mobile Jews pushed out into new areas to make way for new immigrants. In the 1920s Constance Harris was typical of the time in not quite knowing what to think: '(the Jews) move as an unstoppable force towards their goal… However much you dislike them yet we cannot fail to admire their tenacity of purpose, their industry and love for their children, qualities which the average parent in Bethnal Green often lacks.' More explicit anti-Semitism was openly expressed. Bishop Paget in 1921 described the Jewish presence in Spitalfields thus. '(The aliens) occupy at once every house they can secure. Quick-witted, indefatigable, alert, they slip into our places, they take our houses, they sometimes seem to get our work. Certainly I have no hostility for the alien as such. I am sure it is wrong to judge and condemn them *en masse*. I can do more than point to what seems to me the real seriousness of allowing a great piece of London like this, the natural home of thousands and thousands of our hardest workers, to be taken from them, driven out as they are by the constant invasion of people of other races.' By the 1940s, the invasion metaphor had largely disappeared from respectable public debate, but Robb discovered it alive and well in the heart of London.

Anti-Semitism was not ignored by other observers. Self noted wrily that many people identified the true youth movement in Bethnal Green as the Young Fascists. He judged that about 20% of the population were Jewish, '…mainly traders and workers in the clothing industry. They do not constitute the same social and economic problem as in neighbouring Stepney, where they are much more numerous, but they do give rise to difficulties in times of crisis, when feeling can be stirred up against them. In the absence of provocative elements, they are not looked on as foreigners, though they possess some of the best jobs and, as elsewhere in the East End, Jewish landlords are said to be bad landlords.' *Family and Kinship*, by contrast, passes over the Jewish population almost entirely and even seems to deny it a place in the borough. 'Contrary to a general impression, the great majority of the people were Gentiles; according to our survey only about eight per cent of the population was Jewish.' Jewish educational aspirations are mentioned in passing but nothing is said about anti-Semitism.

Comparing the various pictures of Bethnal Green's working class painted in the 1940s and 1950s brings you inevitably to the question of whether they are all compatible. Were the Bethnal Greeners a warm and stable village community sustained by strong kinship loyalties; or were they locked into an inward-looking group culture which produced chronically insecure individuals, predisposed towards violent psychosis? Contemplating this brings you inevitably to the Kray brothers, the career-criminal twins whose lives and mythologies were, and remain, inextricably entangled with Bethnal Green. The Krays have all of Bethnal Green's good blood and bad blood: the fierce family loyalties, the childhood ambitions shaped by the Repton boxing club, the suspicion of outsiders, the aggressive self-sufficiency, the key role played by the 'Mum'. Are the Krays heroes or villains? It is surprisingly difficult to find a consensus, given that they were by any standards violent psychopaths. Despite the brutality of their life-stories, the Krays retain the allure of being working-class heroes, East Enders who carried their culture and authority to the West End and enforced their demands for respect. The *East London Advertiser* still carries the occasional letter protesting that there is still maybe something to admire about the Krays.

In the late 1940s the Kray family moved to a terrace house in Vallance Road at the heart of Bethnal Green, which is where the twins grew up, playing in the street, filching sweets from the shops on Bethnal Green Road and dipping in and out of the local youth club run by nearby Oxford House. On the surface the family must have seemed utterly typical and it is intriguing to wonder whether any member of the Kray family was ever approached by a social researcher, eager to uncover some new nugget of truth about the English people proper.

Overleaf: Off Parmiter Street, 1986. Peter Marshall.

ART

'I was looking for "an image" by which I suppose I meant something that suggested an imaginative world.'

Nigel Henderson, recalling his time in Bethnal Green, 1947–51.

The Krays are one channel through which the world of 1950s Bethnal Green still echoes today. *Family and Kinship* is perhaps another. But if one had to add a third way in which the borough projected itself into the future it would be via the less obvious medium of the visual arts. Bethnal Green played a small but significant role in the fertilisation of post-war ideas and moods that were to prove as durable in highbrow culture as the tower blocks were to be in the urban landscape. It was a site where the 'parallels of life and art', to use the title of a 1953 exhibition at the Institute of Contemporary Arts, were reflected on and turned to creative account. Arguably, it was the encounter with art practice that raised the cultural status of Bethnal Green in the long term; just as much as the encounter with sociological research raised it in the short term.

The key person in this encounter is the artist-photographer Nigel Henderson who moved with his social-anthropologist wife Judith to the Bow end of Bethnal Green in 1947. She had been appointed by J.L. Peterson of University House to run the course 'Discover your Neighbour'. This was a cross-class bridge-building exercise, designed for local professionals to bring them up to speed with the value systems of the people they would be working among. It aimed to explain how historical conditions had created over time 'a cohesive system of attitudes, sympathies, prejudices – what you like', and to encourage professionals to take such value systems seriously. 'To fly in the face of such a system of attitudes and beliefs or to be unconscious or indifferent to their existence would be to render your work among such people useless.' The Hendersons moved into a dilapidated terrace house in Chisenhale Road, where Judith Henderson got to know her neighbours, the Samuels, who had eight children, an uncertain income and who 'could not understand why we, who obviously come from a different background, should want to settle down in a place like this'. While Judith taught her course, she also sent reports about the Samuels back to Tom Harrison of Mass Observation.

Nigel also observed but for his own purposes. During the war Henderson had suffered some sort of psychiatric breakdown. He enrolled in the Slade School after the war, intending to become some sort of artist, but felt little inclination to take formal art education seriously, spending his time instead wandering around the East End looking at things. 'I drew a lot but with no facility at all. It was like running up hill for me.' The loan of a camera was a catalyst. 'It occurred to me to take the Leica around with me on my compulsive walks about the East End; for walking around, always taking streets unfamiliar to me had become a soothing experience for a restless and anxious mind.' The photography habit proved equally compulsive and Henderson began to build up a formidable body of work capturing the surreal landscape of the bomb-damaged East End and the people whose world this was. 'I would think of the small box-like houses and this as a sort of stage set against people were more or less unconsciously acting.' From 1949 to 1952 he produced many thousands of negatives of his East End neighbourhood.

Henderson was fascinated by the physicality of his surroundings. His Bethnal Green photographs dwell on what has been called 'the calligraphy of decay'. He himself described what attracted his eye: 'the slicks and patches of tar on the roads, the cracks and slicks and erosive marks on pavement slabs, the ageing of wood and paintwork, the rich layering of billboards'. Although Henderson photographed what he saw, his pictures were not merely documentary. Many of his negatives were worked on in the darkroom, adding debris from bomb-sites to produce more surreal 'photograms' and collages, often in collaboration with his close friend Eduardo Paolozzi. Paolozzi was a frequent visitor to the Henderson's Bethnal Green home, and he too was curious about their working-class neighbours, as Judith Henderson recorded in 1947. 'Eduardo came over to supper with us. He and Nigel went over to the Samuels' house: the boys were greatly impressed by his strength. He was rather shocked by the atmosphere of dirt and untidiness which was worse than he had expected.'

Perhaps the most famous product of Henderson and Paolozzi's encounter with the post-war East End was the installation 'Patio and Pavilion' created for the Whitechapel Art Gallery's 1956 exhibition, *This Is Tomorrow*. This seminal exhibition provided a menu of possible futures for art, as defined by the new generation of artists, sculptors and architects. As the catalogue promised, '(exhibits) range from orthodox abstract art, with its classical regularity and rational order, through room-size sculptures to walk through, to crazy-house structures plastered with pin-up images from the popular press.' The only common ground between the exhibiters was their belief that art must engage with the modern world of mass culture and post-atomic angst. Whatever the style or theory, the artists all agreed that 'the doors of the Ivory Tower are wide open'.

'Patio and Pavilion' was the creation of Group 6, which included, besides Henderson and Paolozzi, the two architects, Alison and Peter Smithson. The installation was based on the memory of the Hendersons' own unkempt back garden and archetypal Bethnal Green backyards, with their pigeon lofts, corrugated iron and assorted junk. The whole exhibit was intended to communicate the basic human needs for habitat and shelter together with the more mysterious forces of decay and regeneration that shaped people's lives. The structure, 'the Pavilion', had been designed by the Smithsons who departed for an international conference once they had constructed it, leaving Henderson and Paolozzi to fill the empty space and the

'Patio' outside with signs of human habitation. This they achieved through covering the floor of the Patio with sand and scattering *objects trouvés* across every surface, from bits of brick, stone and plaster to metal cog-wheels and mysterious pieces of scrap metal. Inside the Pavilion, which most people read as a garden shed, the viewer was confronted with a massive, giant head, the collage 'Head of a Man' by Henderson. It was the brooding presence of the head that set the mood of the piece as a slightly nihilistic one. 'One could not help feeling', reflected Reyner Banham, that this particular garden shed with its rusted bicycle wheels, a battered trumpet and other homely junk, had been excavated after an atomic holocaust.' Colin St. John Wilson was also impressed but slightly bemused. 'The most striking image in the whole exhibition was Nigel Henderson's giant head (which I later bought from him), though what the hell it was doing in a potting shed I never understood.'

Of all the possible artistic futures on display at the Whitechapel in 1956, the one that made quickest headway in mainstream British art was Pop Art. By the end of the decade the shiny colours and visual tricks of mass-market culture, as represented in the Whitechapel exhibition by Robbie the Robot and Richard Hamilton, had come into their own, leaving the calligraphy of urban decay slightly out of step with the zeitgeist. However in the long term, the Patio and Pavilion aesthetic with its fragments, decaying scraps and personal archaeologies proved a durable strain in British art. As the swinging sixties faded away and the post-industrial dereliction of the 1970s took up where the post-war bomb-sites had left off, so the East End mood rose to the surface once more. By then, this was as much a matter of urban geography as artistic trends. From the 1970s onwards young artists began to colonise the condemned terraces and derelict factories of the post-industrial East End for cheap homes and studios. And perhaps inevitably their surroundings began to seep into their work; sometimes very directly, as with the case of Rachel Whiteread's *House* of 1993, an inside-out cast of a demolished terrace house. Whether consciously or not, many of this generation of artists were reworking the mood of a certain sort of 1950s sensibility, categorised by Alison and Peter Smithson as 'the as found aesthetic'. '[This] was something we thought we named in the early 1950s when we first knew Nigel Henderson and saw his photographs, a perceptive recognition of the actuality around his house in Bethnal Green: children's pavement play-graphics; repetition of "kind" in doors used as site hoardings; the items in the detritus on bombed sites such as the old boot, heaps of nails, fragments of sack and mesh and so on... Thus the "as found" was a new seeing of the ordinary, an openness as to how prosaic "things" could re-energise our inventive activity. A confronting recognition of what the post-war world actually was like.'

The 'as found aesthetic' could conceivable be read unsympathetically as a classic middle class 'appropriation' of working-class wretchedness. If Young and Willmott can be accused of romanticising the working-class family, isn't Henderson guilty of aestheticising the working-class backyard, making poverty picturesque, and imposing a narrative of existential suffering onto a culture he was merely observing. An alternative thought is that Henderson's work provided another way in to the working-class experience, allowing it be inspirational and genuinely spiritual in a way that had not been allowed before. In this reading Henderson gave Bethnal Green a universality that built genuinely new bridges between us and them. This was not just a place for mechanistic urban processes, but somewhere for reflection and inspiration, a place where inner demons could be wrestled with more eloquently than in Hampstead, and where the imaginative world could be discovered and savoured. Or in the words of Bert Smith, Chisenhale Road's knife and scissor-grinder who befriended Henderson, 'if I were asked to describe Nigel I'd say he can talk about a piece of rotten wood and you'd see colours of the rainbow in the very grain'.

In the context of this book, Rachel Whiteread's *House* can be whole-heartedly located within the Bethnal Green universe. It exudes Bethnal Green-ness, not only because her monumental artwork was sited within the boundaries of the old metropolitan borough (Wennington Green where *House* was created is a few streets away from Chisenhale Road), but also because of its rich Bethnal Green resonances. *House* spoke profoundly of encounters between us and them. It was mysterious, impenetrable to the outsider and yet grimly reminiscent of things familiar and homely. It was life-encrusted ground rendered ghostly and dry, human life solidified into a monument. It was presence made absent, colour made grey, high challenge but low threat. Like the Bethnal Green creation it was, *House* conjured into life a fiercely individualist awkward bugger in the shape of Sid Gale, the previous owner of the house, who refused to budge: 'This is my home. I live here,' he wrote on the wall. The official story of *House* was supremely an encounter between us and them, and one which turned hostile, with the final bout 'won' by Bethnal Green. If the 'as found aesthetic' was a middle-class appropriation, then Bethnal Green certainly had its revenge in 1993 by destroying *House,* by command of the Bow Neighbourhood Council. The demolition attracted howls of protest from the art world who saw it as cultural vandalism of the highest order. The Chair of the Arts Council, Peter Palumbo, called the locals 'dunces'. At about the same time Tower Hamlets' neighbourhood system of local government had thrown up a British National Party councillor on the Isle of Dogs; but, judging by the quantity of column inches in the broadsheets, the demolition of *House* was the more alarming example of the dangers of placing power in the hands of the people. If *House* was an archetypal Bethnal Green artwork, its destruction marked an archetypal Bethnal Green moment. The goal, much talked about in the 1950s, of Bethnal Green shaking off external support to take control of its own affairs, was achieved triumphantly and with flying colours. From the Bethnal Green point of view *House* was all about us rather than them.

Overleaf: Old Ford Road, 2005. Peter Marshall.

5 BACK TO THE PARISH

'The East End cockney community is a dynamic group of hard working people connected by history, friendship, marriage and traditions which have been passed down generation to generation. This area of London is our birthright. We live here'.

Edward Ponsonby , letter to the *East London Advertiser*, February 2005.

For the last ten years or so, Edward Ponsonby of Bethnal Green has been one of the most prolific correspondents to the *East London Advertiser*. Early in 2005 the sitting MP for Bethnal Green and Bow, Oona King, made the mistake of doubting his existence. It was perhaps an easy mistake to make. His regular letters had a whiff of central casting about them ('in my opinion it was this firm and decisive action by Ron and Reg which had the effect of transforming East London into a clean delightful and safe area in which to bring up our children all these years ago'), and he had recently popped up in the chatroom of www.politicalbetting.com, although this Edward Ponsonby turned out to be an identity thief. However Edward Ponsonby did exist and he was exactly what his letters suggested – an old-school cockney, a hard line believer in the East End as a land apart, given to the working classes by royal decree way back in the mists of time. Ponsonby is what sociologists call a 'cultural essentialist' and his habit of preaching cockney essentialism in the letter pages of the *East London Advertiser* has been a regular feature of the paper for the last few years, even to the degree that other letter writers accuse him of over-egging the cockney cake: 'Not that I don't find Ponsonby entertaining,' said Norman Sampson. 'Don't get me wrong, as a cockney myself I am all for defending this dying breed but find other subjects to write about, like pensions for example.'

But Edward Ponsonby seems to have been taken aback by the general election of May 2005. This was a classic Bethnal Green moment. The national spotlight shone dazzlingly on the place as Oona King gathered her forces to fight off the challenge from George Galloway, erupting into the political mainstream like a garrulous character from nineteenth-century fiction, florid of face and vocabulary, dripping the gall and galloping egotism that his name promised. The East End likes a character, but – as even his supporters admitted – George wasn't very Bethnal Green. As Galloway's voice rose, so Ponsonby's fell. In February the *East London*

Left: Club Row, 2005.

Advertiser printed a letter from the cockney fundamentalist restating his credo that 'this area of London is our birthright', but this turned out to be virtually Ponsonby's last pronouncement. Perhaps the newspaper decided not to print his letters. After all there were a lot of voices that needed to be heard in the run up to the May 2005 election. Feelings ran high. The election was not just about politics, it was also about the identity and soul of Bethnal Green, its past and future. Bethnal Green had last elected a non-Labour MP in the 1930s when the Liberal Sir Percy Harris completed his long run of election victories in Bethnal Green South West. Since then the various Bethnal Green seats had been rock-solid Labour / Co-operative and the old tribal loyalties were assumed by many to be sufficiently robust as to withstand any winds of change. Galloway swept into Bethnal Green triumphant in his discovery that 40% of the electorate were of Bengali origin, throwing open his big tent of being anti-everything that smacked of authority, government or American imperialism. The old working class and the new gentrifiers were all wrong-footed. He was a love or hate figure, depending on age and experience. In my tower block opinion was divided. Some thought he was a people's hero. Others, including me, read him as a crypto-fascist. If that man gets in I'm moving out, I said – a foolish hostage to fortune which I now regret.

Whatever Edward Ponosnby thought about Galloway, other correspondents to the *East London Advertiser* understood that his campaign changed Bethnal Green's image in the outside world and shook its own sense of itself. Any lingering beliefs in the old East End homogeneity evaporated, leaving behind a Babylonian confusion of fragmented identities where ethnicities, religions and values criss-crossed each other noisily and angrily. As John Rush, another correspondent colourfully summarised it, 'the race card is being thrown into the ring more often than knickers at a Tom Jones concert. The Lib Dems don't want a Cockney candidate but a Bengali flaunting their views down the Bethnal Green 'Frog and Toad'. The Conservatives in their politically-correct wisdom also plumped for a Bangladeshi candidate. Labour have a Scotsman in an aging Celtic shirt and a half-Jewish woman prone to anti-Semitic orations parading the streets telling us how good it is to be loved by them... Meanwhile Respect's Big Chief Talking Bull, Bonnie Dundee George Galloway... by Sunday afternoon he's knocking doors in Dhaka High Street in Bangladesh. No-one south of Dundee has ever understood him, apart from a couple of psychiatrists. So what chance the people of Bangladesh, lumbered with a geographically challenged 'Jock' who has aspired to be a Cockney since a foetus. Am I the only Catholic to support abortion?'. As the writer, a cockney 'but also a Jock!', understood: things in Bethnal Green definitely ain't what they used to be.

Brick Lane Market, 1986. Peter Marshall.

DEATH

'One of the biggest names in East End menswear is closing down after 80 years. Now Sternfeld's – specialising in the 'outsize' – is shutting shop for the last time at the end of the month. The business opened in 1924 in the busy Green Street, what is now Bethnal Green's famous Roman Road.'

East London Advertiser, 1 September, 2005.

For me, the May 2005 election also co-incided with writing the last chapter of this book. I had sketched the story-line out during the Christmas break of 2004 and thought I knew where I wanted to take it. The romance, I was going to say, lives on. Despite multiculturalism, gentrification, de-industrialisation, post de-industrialisaton, the end of modernism, the possible death of class and all those other things that have happened to London since Bethnal Green's glory days in the 1950s, Bethnal Green's old stories still had currency. Bethnal Green, I would suggest, even despite the demographic revolution that had left its citizens fluent Bengali speakers, retained its position as a distinctive and special place: an oasis of romantic, oriental otherness, shimmering with promise and quickened by pity; a place of outsiders and authenticity, offering an irresistible alchemy of high challenge and low threat; a place where seekers of urban treasure would find meaningful maps.

Suddenly I wasn't so sure that I believed this. The ground was shifting. I began to consider whether stretching the metaphor of romance into the present day was even possible, let alone worthwhile. The most obvious conclusion to the book, now I came to think about it, was that the romance of Bethnal Green, far from being alive and well, was well and truly over. The place had served its purpose as a place of cultural encounter between us and them and now the capital had moved on. The old stories of derring-do, of intrepid explorers crossing chasms so that rich met poor and west met east, were passing into myth. New stories were being written and just as modernism had given way to multiculturalism, so romance had now led to divorce. The Galloway episode was perhaps the exception that proved the rule that Bethnal Green was no longer a highly charged place in the national imagination. The old parish and borough boundaries had lost their power to shape memories and perhaps the old stories of place were now little more than comforters for sentimental oldies.

Another possibility was that the romance conducted in Bethnal Green between us and them over the last two centuries had turned into a marriage. Bethnal Green and the metropolitan middle classes had come together in wedlock and evened-up their differences. In cultural terms, it could be said that this evening-up has seen the middle classes move ever more admiringly towards the old working-class way of life. For the moment at least, everyone wants to be like the common people. Sunday markets are a case in point. Once a working-class phenomenon, Brick Lane, Columbia Road and Spitalfields markets have today been clasped to middle-class hearts. Going to the pub and eating takeaway food no longer have shameful associations of working-class poverty. Offal and faggots have been elevated to British cuisine (jellied eels remain a dish too far). Top hats have passed into history but cloth caps are still going strong. Behaviours traditionally associated with the working class – speaking your mind, not standing on ceremony, swearing – have moved to the middle-class mainstream, a change that probably would have astonished the university students billeted in Oxford House during the 1930s. 'I remember early on' recalled one of the locals, 'they didn't even understand the swearing, and somebody rather innocent was complaining bitterly as he walked down the steps from upstairs, having listened to the boys. "I don't know, what does that mean when they say f…ing, f…ing, f…ing and all that?" And he'd never heard it before you see.'

A third possibility was that the romance has turned unpleasantly sour as the 'them' mantle, far from being appropriated by the well-off, has slipped back onto the shoulders of the poor. In this scenario, the working class has been cruelly duped: welcomed into society in the 1950s with promises of the Welfare State and full employment, only to be rudely ejected within a generation, their jobs taken from them and the Welfare State given to others. Rebranded against their will as 'white', the working classes are back out in the cold as the Cinderellas, condemned to a life of drab drudgery and never going to the ball. Whatever one's views about this way of looking at things, it is not difficult to detect a sense of loss in the Bethnal Green psyche. Edward Ponsonby is not the only correspondent to the *East London Advertiser* voicing this mood. Something has gone and the loss is perceived as unjust, in that it has been taken away, rather than freely given. The blame is placed not so much at the doors of the new Bethnal Greeners for taking, but at the authorities for giving. The multicultural present is dammed as the unnaturally monstrous creation of the Baron Frankenstein-like authorities whose culpability in grafting the 'them' of the newcomers onto the 'us' of the indiginous settlers is at best a mistake and at worst a deliberate betrayal. The letters often express an uneasy joviality, as if the writer is struggling with the balance between asserting rights and not giving offence. 'The East End's "Englishness" is disappearing as the relentless creeping ivy of multiculturalism strangles the rose in the garden of political correctness' wrote G. Cope from Stepney. 'How long will it be before it will be an offence to sing Knees Up Mother Brown because it could incite violence against female Asian elders?… I don't expect immigrants to scoff jellied eels and listen to Chas and Dave – we'd all probably be better off if they jellied Chas and Dave and asked the eels to give a song. But a serious attempt at learning English would be a start.'

The loss being mourned is perhaps the loss of difference that made the working class so distinctive. For previous generations, the cockneys were the ones who were 'colourful' and exotic. They were the orientals, their street markets often likened to eastern bazaars as a way of conveying their life and vitality: Club Row was 'a bit of Baghdad' to H.V. Morton in the 1920s; Sclater Street was like a Cairo souk. In the twenty-first century, the social cachet attached to cultural difference has never been higher but the cockneys have fallen victim to bad timing because they are no longer the most attractive or exotic 'them'. There are now real orientals to add colour to the streets. The Bengali community brings to London a traditional cuisine of freshwater fish and exotic vegetables, hand-crafted pots, colourful fabrics and a sense of the wide horizons of the global village. All the cockneys can offer is tinned food and a sense of island Britain imprisoned in its white past. Cockney culture is now deemed to be 'white' and a bit too one-dimensional, the sing-songs and pearly kings and queens passed over as not quite different enough. The nineteenth century ran two co-existing stereotypes of the Bethnal Green poor – the long-suffering saintly victim, to be treated with compassion, and the semi-criminalized rough to be treated more harshly. Maybe, today, echoes of both stereotypes persist with the 'white' working class tending to be confined to the ruffian one.

One of the few traditional East End public ceremonies that survives on the streets is the funeral processions managed by the famous Bethnal Green funeral parlour W.E. English & Son. On these occasions an elaborately decorated Victorian glass-sided hearse is drawn through the streets by black horses with black plumes, followed by a slow fleet of shiny black Mercedes. It is always a powerful sight, a sombre and melancholy *memento mori*, if you feel in contemplative mood. There are several public events celebrating the arrival of new cultures but few to grieve for the passing of an old. The public funeral is probably the nearest thing old Bethnal Green gets to a cultural ritual as its old ways pass into myth and theatre.

This was certainly the conclusion many drew from the most magnificent examples of all such occasions in recent years, the funerals of Charlie and Reggie Kray in April and October 2000. 'There was an overwhelming sense of faded grandeur, a attempt to relive a way of life gone by,' was typical of the sentiments expressed by most of the journalists from the national newspapers who came to cover the events. Reading these accounts, it was impossible not to reflect on the resonances with the events in 1872 which marked the opening of the Bethnal Green Museum. Then, as now, journalists came to marvel at the tribe of 'metropolitan orientals' and the strange way they dressed. Whereas in 1872 what caught the journalists eyes was the 'frank and homely' cotton print frocks and shirt-sleeves, this time it was the glitz. 'They glittered in the sun,' exclaimed William Leith in the *Evening Standard*. 'Their outfits were elaborate, shiny. Everybody was buffed. Parts of them looked crispy.' The jewellery and accessories came in for particular comment. 'The shoes! I've never seen a richer selection of men's shoes as I saw at Charlie Kray's funeral. A lot of these shoes were effectively slippers. They weren't meant for walking great distances. These are guys who delegate. One man was wearing Versace pumps, the sort of footwear a Sultan might wear, made of fine brown suede cut low with a lot of foot showing.' There was even a mild re-run of the Bethnal Green slander as respectable Bethnal Greeners angrily asserted their wish not to be represented by unpleasant stereotypes. 'Sir, I find it insulting to all the thousands of decent, honest Bethnal Green citizens, among whom I've lived very happily for over 50 years, to read Dick Hobbs in his obituary of Reg Kray repeat the popular myth that 'squalor' in the East End bred criminals. On the contrary, I know that adversity in hard times bred hard-working, brave, humorous and kind men and women. RIP the Kray legend.' A 13 year old boy took the *Evening Standard* to task for describing the streets of Bethnal Green as 'shabby'. 'I have lived here all my life and I find this an insult to the people who live here. Maybe Tower Hamlets is known to be a bit poor, but Bethnal Green is a nice place to live and 'shabby' is an unfair adjective to use when describing it.'

Brick Lane Mela, 2006. Peter Marshall.

LIFE

I live in Bethnal Green and I love its diversity. There's a big student population in East London, whilst Brick Lane, Spitalfields Market and Shoreditch are just a stone's throw away. It feels alive.'

Kele Okereke, in The Times, February 2005.

So 2005 brought the suspicion that the old romance of Bethnal Green was either over, sour or dead. And all the way through 2005 there seemed to be very good reasons for coming round to the point of view that Bethnal Green was undergoing a thorough de-Bethnal Greening. The old stories of poor weavers, slum housing, costermongers and philanthropists had not fully disappeared but they were fading into a ghostly shadow land, difficult to map onto the present day topography of the multicultural city. The Bethnal Green that appeared in the press and on the television, as the Oona King v George Galloway boxing match grew ever more compelling, was not unrecognisable but neither was it familiar. 'The second most Islamic constituency in the country,' said the *Times* in April. In early May *Newsnight* brought Salam Pax 'the Baghdad blogger' to London to report on the way the British conduct their elections and he chose to go to the constituency where he felt he would have most affinity with the issues and the people, which was Bethnal Green and Bow. George Galloway triumphed and Bethnal Green's new image was here to stay, thanks in no small part to the events that followed later in the year. Two months after the election, London experienced the 7th of July bombings, which despite the Mayor's admirable 'one London' campaign, disturbed deep currents in the East End's sense of itself. As the working class had become the white working class, so now the Bangladeshi Bethnal Greeners became the Islamic community. And Bethnal Green, in the media's eyes, become an Islamic village where the parish pump issues were very firmly global.

There were a lot of statistics bandied about in 2005 and they all underlined that Bethnal Green's new image was not just a media invention. By the time of the 2005 election roughly 40,000 of the electorate of Bethnal Green and Bow were categorised as Bengali. As with many parts of inner London, the population change had happened quickly. In 1951 the census had recorded 800 people of Pakistani birth in the whole of Tower Hamlets, most at that time living in Stepney. By 2001 the census recorded 65,553 East Enders who defined themselves as Bengali, most tracing their origin back to the Sylheti region of Bangladesh. The five wards that roughly corresponded to the territory of the old borough of Bethnal Green had a population made up of 54% white, 36% Aisan / Bengali, 6% Black, 2% Chinese and 2% other. More telling of change than the statistics is the figure of Baroness Uddin of Bethnal Green who was raised to the peerage in 1998. In the 1950s it might conceivably have been forseen that before the end of the century someone from Bethnal Green would emerge from the community to take the name to the House of Lords, but it would have taken a very far-sighted prophet to predict that this would be a Bangladeshi woman. Pola Uddin was not strictly the first Bethnal Greener to enter the house of Lords. Bernard Delfont, born Boris Winogradsky, had become Lord Delfont of Stepney in 1976. His life story had taken him from a childhood in the Boundary Street Estate, following his family's arrival in 1912 as Russian speaking 'aliens'. Baroness Uddin was also distantly preceded by George John Shaw-Lefevre, a grandee of Huguenot descent who had assumed the title Lord Eversley of Old Ford in 1906. But Pola Uddin's Bethnal Green title was a first, as were other aspects of her remarkable journey through British society. Not only the first Bangladeshi-born Briton to enter the House of Lords, she was also the first Muslim woman and the first peer to swear her oath of allegiance in the name of her own faith.

But the sea change in Bethnal Green's identity in 2005 wasn't just a matter of the district's new Bengali face. The other great urban force roaming the territory in the East End over the last decade has been gentrification and that also sprung some surprises in 2005. In November 2005 it was reported that the average salary in the parliamentary constituency of Bethnal Green and Bow was £42,956 putting it fourth in the list of top-earners' constituencies across London (Poplar and Canning Town, which includes Docklands, was top with £78,901). This news caused a predictable flurry in the pages of the *East London Advertiser*, with some correspondents denouncing the statistics as false and an insult to the real Bethnal Greeners. Extending the statistics nationally made Tower Hamlets the top borough in the country for high-wage earners: again, a statistic greeted with incredulity by many locals who no doubt remembered that nine years earlier, the very same newspapers reported that Tower Hamlets had overtaken Hackney as the most deprived borough in the country where half of all households lived on a weekly income of £150. The view at ground level, where poverty among real Bethnal Greeners is still very much in evidence, does indeed cast suspicion on the wealth statistics, but here I should perhaps admit to my own role in the puzzle. The real Bethnal Greener, according to the National Office of Statistics, is me. For the past few years they have been ringing me up regularly as one of only two people to supply data related to employment – including salary – for this particular E2 postcode. When they first rang, I tried to demur on the grounds that I really was not typical and they would get a much more truthful picture of E2 by asking someone else. However they insisted that truth was exactly what random selection guaranteed.

Neither of today's Bethnal Greens – Bengali Bethnal Green nor gentrified Bethnal Green – sits altogether comfortably with the old Bethnal Green. Despite Tower Hamlets council's best efforts to jazz up Bethnal Green's diversity credentials, it has been hard to find a good fit between the old stories and the new. Immigration and cultural diversity is not really part of Bethnal Green's repertoire of old stories. In the East End, Stepney is the place that has always carried the standard for exotic other races. Stepney was London's 'coloured quarter', as the title of a 1953 book described it. Cable Street was 'London's Harlem' with a café culture that included Maltese, West Indian, Pakistani, Greek and Italian establishments. 'Stepney is the coloured man's district', said the author in 1953, 'they have occupied it and made it their own'. By contrast Bethnal Green in 1953 was busy being an English village. There was a somewhat hidden history of individuals with dark skins who helped steer local life. In the 1890s Bethnal Green had been represented by a Conservative MP of Indian birth, Mancherjee Merwanjee Bhownaggree. In the 1940s the folk-hero of the Bethnal Green 1943 tube disaster was Dr Baldev Kaushal, a Punjabi-born local GP who ignored his own injuries to minister to others. These however were the individual exceptions to the general rule that in Bethnal Green the only racial divisions that broke surface were between Jews, Irish and English.

Statistically, the change came in the 1960s and 1970s (particularly following the Bangladeshi war for independence in 1971), by which time the growing numbers of Bengali families in Spitalfields, squashed into old sub-standard properties had begun to attract serious attention from the authorities as suitable cases for help. Here at last was a way of co-opting the new arrivals into the old stories. Here was a new group of people with outsider status, cut off from mainstream society by a variety of deprivations, unfairly discriminated against as individuals because of group stereotypes, manifestly poor and defined by a geographical place. The analogies between the twentieth-century Bengalis and the nineteenth-century poor were apparent to many observers. And there seems little doubt that life in an overcrowded London tenement could be as harsh and dispiriting for Bangladeshi families in the 1970s as it had been for destitute weavers in the 1860s or Yiddish-speaking Russians in the 1890s. Many of the same patterns remerged. The outsider group had virtues of strong family links, entrepreneurial drive and a mutually supportive culture but these could also produce exclusiveness and insularity. They liked living in the place and were cemented into the locality by occupation: a 1995 survey found that 36% of the Bangladeshi residents in the Bethnal Green City Challenge area actually worked in the local area, as compared to only 18% of the white residents. There were some cultural habits about 'them' that the 'us' of mainstream English society found difficult to accommodate. Reaction to the difference that they so obviously represented repeated the pattern of much of what had gone before, including violence. In what could be loosely seen as re-runs of the anti-Irish riots of the eighteenth century and the anti-Jewish demonstrations of the nineteenth century, the 1970s saw the notorious National Front marches in Brick Lane. In 1978 a local garment worker, Altab Ali, was murdered.

The recognition of an old pattern taking shape was undoubtedly a spur to action for Tower Hamlets council who in the 1980s and 1990s addressed the task of engineering out otherness, both through their own housing allocation procedures, which had been an unwitting source of discrimination on the ground, and the active deployment of cultural and economic strategies reinforcing the message that these people were the new face of us rather than the new face of them. At the Spitalfields end of Bethnal Green 'Banglatown' was invented by the council in the early 1990s as a branding exercise to market the Brick Lane curry houses in the face of the encroaching City property developers. Despite insisting that 'Banglatown' was not a 'culturally essentialist' title, merely an umbrella term beneath which other visitor attractions could flourish, it has not worked quite in that way. On the ground the name has lost out to its unofficial equivalent, 'Brick Lane'. Happily, the signs all point to the council having done a fair job in steering this part of Tower Hamlets away from a future that delivers the problems of the past. Educationally, Bangladeshi children are doing well in local schools. The community has rooted very strongly; it has six newspaper, one dating back to 1969. Bengali-speakers are active in local politics and the first-generation millionaires are already moving out of the area to country mansions, following the path long-trodden by London merchants of all creeds since the seventeenth century.

One can also find some faint echos of the old stories in today's gentrification story. Just as Nigel Henderson in the 1940s had found Bethnal Green a psychologically comfortable place for his outsider sensibilities, so too did the artists and squatters of the late 1960s and 1970s, who arrived in the East End signed up to the counter-culture, and workers solidarity. But even for them, and more so for the middle-class migrants who came after, the dynamic was not quite the same. Middle-class migration is now less a story about romantic outsiderness and more a story about property. In the old days the rich west imported new buildings into the property-poor east; now the east has the property surplus and is pulling the property-poor westerners eastwards with the lure of affordable housing. Bethnal Green's post-war flats and maisonettes were built to be the New Jerusalem but have become, thanks to right-to-buy legislation, an estate agent's paradise. 'The vibrant and cosmopolitan nature of Bethnal Green and its surrounding areas,' exclaims one local firm, 'is mirrored in the types of properties available locally for both sales and lettings. Within any 100 yard radius you will find every conceivable type of housing from modern to period and from purpose built to conversions. There truly is something for everyone.' The housing market in Bethnal Green is a hot one and, according to Tower Hamlets council, if right-to-buy activity continues at its present level, there will be very little social housing left in the borough in four years time. Again, I have to confess to an interest here. My tower block was one of the last built by the metropolitan borough. Tower Hamlets sold it off in the early 1990s to a property developer and since then it has been lived in by owner-occupiers and their tenants, a typically-London, globally-assorted, mixture of people mainly under 40: professionals, students, medics and a few families with babies.

The invasion of the gentrifiers is a subtle one. Some might say the best adjective is stealth. Buildings remain standing: the Approach pub is still a pub, albeit also an art gallery and gastropub. In November 2005 its crab cakes with mango mayonnaise helped win it a place in the *Good Food Guide*. The old Cheshire Street municipal bath-house looks roughly the same on the outside but the building has been turned into flats and now has a metal fence around it protecting the cars parked on the forecourt. Just along the street, the row of Victorian shops continue to house local shops for local people, but now the products are luxury leather handbags, Finnish design and cool hair cuts. The splendid 1888 red-brick fire station on Roman Road is now the London Buddhist Centre. Former light-industrial premises now house cutting-edge art galleries and studios. Inside, the 'as found aesthetic' is going from strength to strength. 'A lot of the work we do at Artlab follows the same philosophy,' said one Bethnal Green artist to the *Independent*, in a Me and My Home property feature. 'The acquisition of "found objects" is important. We have used taxi seats from our friends at Cyprus Taxis down the road, in some of our sculpture and have also made some chandeliers / sculptures from found cable reel.' The new Bethnal Greeners blend into the old background: they wear fleeces and trainers, they queue up to buy vegetables from market stalls and ride the number eight bus. Some even have old greyhounds as pets. But their arrival can still leave older residents bemused. 'I want to know how all these artists make a living,' asked Harry King, landlord of the Approach pub whose family had run the pub for nearly 100

Overleaf: Roman Road, 1988. Peter Marshall.

years until Harry sold it in 1997. 'There wasn't one gallery or one studio and now we are invaded. We can't see how they make a living apart from teaching.'

Gentrification and multiculturalism were both well embedded into Bethnal Green's social geography by the time I arrived in 1993 but, looking back, it feels as if the cycles of change had then only just begun to roll. In the last ten years, the pace has quickened and Bethnal Green has moved on from the fidgety, floating world it was then. The place feels somehow less empty. The streets feels more cosmopolitan, and more charged with energy, filled as they seem to be with more young people and fewer pensioners - although the latter still tend make their presence felt by shouting. The energy and spark is sometimes palpable. There is a sense of being plugged in. The advent of the mobile phone has revealed that Bethnal Green's new young population is international and the number eight bus often rolls along like a great multilingual chatroom, crackling with the rhythms and cadences of Polish, Spanish, or Mandarin Chinese. But despite the charge of energy, Bethnal Green's mood of constant fidgeting seems to have calmed down since 1993. It no longer feels like a shanty town and the shops in the Bethnal Green Road seem to be more firmly rooted. This is partly thanks to the arrival of high-street chains. In 1993 there was just Tesco, Woolworths and MacDonalds. Now they have been joined by Boots, the Halifax Building Society and a real Kentucky Fried Chicken which replaced one of several ersatz fried chicken takeaways. Towards the Brick Lane end of the Bethnal Green Road a Bank of Asia has opened and NatWest has opened a new branch in Roman Road. The small shops still come and go but even they seem to exhude a rootedness and confidence that was never there before. In 1993 the saree shops were all barricaded in to their premises like wholesalers, their small windows crammed with bolts of cloth so that outsiders couldn't see in. Now a new generation has installed plate glass windows, open to all and revealing inside the light wood floors and elegant displays of brilliantly coloured sarees on mannequins. They are now called 'fashion galleries' or 'plazas' and have been joined by a new breed of equally smart 'exclusive' wedding shops. I may of course be misreading the signs but this all suggests the confidence that comes with affluence. Statistically the Bangladeshi Bethnal Greeners remain one of England's poorest communities but there seems to be money around. Today you see women wearing black burkas in the Bethnal Green Road, a rare sight in 1993, but those who worry about cultural ghettoisation should savour the intoxicating aroma of entrepreneurial pheronomes in the air. The City is getting closer by the year and the Bangladeshi Bethnal Greeners are behaving as Londoners always have done over the centuries, opening shops, trading goods off market stalls, selling commodities to fellow Londoners and making profits. Whether George Galloway likes it or not, capitalism is one of the heady romances that London offers to all, regardless of colour or creed.

ROMANCE

'I have loads of friends who live nearby – such as Jake and Dinos Chapman. It's a high-voltage part of town that has such an exciting dynamic, full of artists, writers, thinkers, waiters, tailors… But what really makes the place so special is the mix of cultures … There is such a great village atmosphere. When new people move in they are just accepted; the locals look out for each other. I know the man in the sweet shop, the guy in the off licence and my greengrocer (thank God we don't have a Tesco on Brick Lane)'.

Tracey Emin, Evening Standard, 25 April 2005.

Walking back home along the Bethnal Green Road early one evening, after drinking a little too much at an exhibition-opening in Shoreditch, I was suddenly overwhelmed with the conviction that I was quite wrong to think that the romance of Bethnal Green had died. It was a summer evening and Bethnal Green was charged with Bethnal Green-ness. The litter drifted along the pavements. Scraps of indeterminate meat and pizza crust lay in the gutter: here a purple plastic children's toy, there an old party streamer. The torn, fly posters on the encrusted brick walls made a richly satisfying collage. Orange street lights glowed; glass windows shimmered with the reflected sunset in the west as cars moved past, their rear red lights forming an intensely pleasing and optimistic pattern. In the distance a dog barked. There were lots of people on the streets. Outside the hairdressers at the top of Brick Lane the usual group of young Japanese were hanging out in their zig-zag hairstyles and stripey socks. I walked on across the life-encrusted pavements, joining in the Bethnal Green passagiata as the sunset waxed and waned. I walked past shops glowing with warm yellow light, encountered Somali elders strolling, and crossed paths with students laden with Tesco bags. The pub doors were open and the number eight bus rolled by like an old, reliable friend. It was a Charles Lamb moment and by the time I got home I was thoroughly overcome with fullness of joy at so much life.

Back home, I made myself a cup of tea and reflected on the thought that the reason I resented George Galloway so much was that his romance was elbowing out mine. Romance was not in fact dead at all, the mood had multiplied so that now everyone had their own personally-customised romance of Bethnal Green. Romance was the new romance. The young Japanese were dreaming their strange fashionista fantasies. The students were backpacking through a fairyland of urban hedonism. The owners of the £million-to-buy Huguenot merchant houses in Spitalfields were lost in a rhapsody of being authentic. The artists were high on the area's energy. Edward Ponsonby was doggedly pursuing the mirage of a cockney Utopia. And Galloway, too, had his heart on his sleeve. Good old Bethnal Green offered him the irresistable mix of Arabian spice and old-school socialism, a creed whose flame, like Ponsonby's cockneyism, burns every brighter as it passes into memory. How could he not fall in love with the place. There is always something unbearable about someone else's romance intruding on your own, as it must inevitably do if the object of affection is the same thing. Whether the romance is with a place or person, the natural reaction is to think that the intruder cannot really understand: theirs is not a true romance but an exercise in personal vanity, a masquerade and a delusion. However cities are by nature promiscuous and those who love them must learn to share the territory, although this is easier said than done.

In Bethnal Green today, despite the occasional turf wars, the general rule is that the various romances, however self-contained, co-exist peacefully and cross-fertilise each other. Pelliccis café on the Bethnal Green Road famously feeds young artists as well as old-time Bethnal Greeners; Kelly's pie and mash shop has a handbill for the National Theatre in its window; the Bengali-run leather shops at the top of Brick Lane provide East Enders with flash leather coats. A few Muslim boys have joined the Repton boxing club. Everyone shops at Tesco, which stocks halal food as it also does pricey South African wine and Sunny Delight. The local newsagents sell *Another Magazine* and the pound shops do great business selling colourful, cheap plastic things from around the world to local people of all tastes and backgrounds. This is the rich mix of the East End as a living kaleidescope, shaken up every now and then but always falling into a harmonious pattern.

I would like to think that the reason for this apparently harmonious co-existence lies in the past, in the common resource of buildings, mood and character which Bethnal Green offers to all its dreaming romantics. All must draw something from the past, even if it is only the vague sense that Bethnal Green, because it has been poor and working-class in the past, now has the virtues of being somehow 'honest' and 'different'. It is not a bad image for a place to have these days; and for those who prefer their identities to be non-mainstream and interestingly different, East London is the place to be. It's a little bit edgy, a little bit real and somehow the transition from pie and mash shops to organic food markets or Sylheti-run takeaways doesn't seem too far a distance for a district to travel. The buildings too are part of the romance and there the past must inevitably quicken the romances of the present. The bricks and mortar of the Bethnal Green Museum and Oxford House, the stone of York Hall and the concrete slabs of Keeling House, all play their part in maintaining and constantly re-calibrating the balance between continuity and change that makes up a sense of place.

Can the balancing action of the past on the present extend its protective effect into the future? Psycho-geographers often muse on the relationship of past and present in London in a melodramatic way, seeing beneath the shiny superficial urbanity of the twenty-first-century city a crusty and unstable geology of ancient memories, myths and dark forces. In Bethnal Green, the global village goes about its daily business among the internet cafes and brightly coloured street furniture of Brick

Lane: but perhaps the filth of Henry Gavin, the brutality of the Krays and the district's genetic predisposition to overcrowding will one day force a darker mood back up to the surface. Personally, I see the psycho-geography of Bethnal Green in a more optimistic way as charging the district with warmth, sentiment, a predisposition for people to be nice to each other and an enviable habit of being content. Here, the last word should go to one of Edward Ponsonby's rivals as cockney-essentialist-in-chief on the *East London Advertiser's* letters page. Beryl Horne's epistles provided living proof that the Bethnal Greeners' habit of seeing the glass half-full was alive and well in the last decade of the twentieth century. In the 1890s Booth's data collectors had recorded Bethnal Green women avowing that there couldn't be a nicer place to live, despite all the tribulations of poverty. 100 years later Beryl Horne echoed the sentiment in a poem.

Ode to Bethnal Green
If ever you go down Bethnal Green Road
You'll see the barrow boys pulling their load.
Puffing and swearing, and sometimes yawning
For they set up their stalls very early each morning.

There is Woolworths, pie and mash and A Tesco store,
We have it all in Bethnal Green, who could ask for more?
We get entertainment over Weavers for our kids,
Where they can run around and blow their lids.

There's a museum with lots of old toys,
Something that's fun for all girls and boys,
You can even go swimming over the York Hall,
This is great fun, for big and the small.

You can even send a message to Between the Lines
I have done this myself oh! So many times
So there's something for everyone, you see what I mean
Never a dull moment here, in good old Bethnal Green.

METROPOLITAN BOROUGH OF BETHNAL GREEN
DELTA ESTATE
THIS STONE WAS LAID BY
THE MAYOR
COUNCILLOR HENRY E. TATE, J.P.
22ND SEPTEMBER 1936
HOUSING COMMITTEE

COUNCILLOR	A. G. CLARK	CHAIRMAN
COUNCILLOR	H. HOOKE	VICE-CHAIRMAN
	THE MAYOR	

ALDERMAN
E. BALME

COUNCILLORS

E. F. BERRY	MRS A. HILLMAN	E. SCHLEICH
MRS M. S. BRIDGER	P. T. JOYCE	G. A. SIMMONDS
P. J. BRIDGER	J. E. A. KING, L.C.C.	W. G. WEBSTER
J. C. EDWARDS	J. J. LECOUNT	H. R. WILSON, J.P.
A. W. HASTINGS	P. O'BRIEN	E. A. WORMALD

E. C. P. MONSON, F.R.I.B.A.
ARCHITECT

DAVID J. KEEP
TOWN CLERK

A. E. DARBY, A.M.I.C.E.
BOROUGH ENGINEER

NOTES

The most comprehensive history of Bethnal Green is found in the Victoria County History's *A History of the county of Middlesex: volume II*, Oxford 1998, edited by T.F.T. Baker.

The following works are quoted throughout:

Charles Booth, *Life and Labour of the People in London*, London 1902. In particular, 3rd series, volume 2; and 1st series, volume 3, chapter 2.

Hector Gavin, *Sanitary Ramblings, being sketches and illustrations of Bethnal Green. A type of the condition of the metropolis and other large towns*, London 1848.

Ruth Glass and Maureen Frankel, *A Profile of Bethnal Green*, Association for Planning and Regional Reconstruction, Report no.39, February 1946. Adapted as 'How they live at Bethnal Green' in *Contact: Britain between West and East*, ed A. G. Weidenfeld and H. de C. Hastings, London 1946.

Constance Harris, *The Use of Leisure in Bethnal Green. A survey of social conditions in the borough, 1925 to 1926*, London 1927.

Percy A. Harris, foreword to *Old Bethnal Green* by George F. Vale, London 1934.

P.J.O. Self 'Voluntary Organisations in Bethnal Green' in *Voluntary Social Services, their place in the modern state*, ed. A.F.C. Bourdillon, London 1945.

Michael Young and Peter Willmott, *Family and Kinship in East London*, London 1957.

OTHER REFERENCES

INTRODUCTION pp. 1–7

5   **'Oxford influences'** quoted in Mandy Ashworth, *The Oxford House in Bethnal Green*, London (Oxford House) 1984 which is also the source of the quote **'We'd never met'**. For Stewart Headlam see F.G. Bettany, *Stewart Headlam: a biography*, 1926. The recent study is *Slumming*, Seth Koven, Princeton 2004.

6   **'Bethnal Green is an exciting place'** Mike Fenton 'Living in Bethnal Green: together or apart' in *London: the Promised Land?*, ed. Anne Kershen, London 1997.

CHAPTER 1 pp. 9–27

DIFFERENCE

11   **'Dense, dingy, poverty-stricken'** G.R. Emerson, *London. How the Great City grew* , London 1862.

11–12   The Blomfield Churches quotes are taken from Hugh McLeod, *Class and Religion in the Late Victorian City*, London 1974 and Booth.

13   The Columbia Market quotes are from Booth and Nikolaus Pevsner, *The Buildings of England, London II*, London 1952.

13   **'Bethnal Green is certainly'** *Saturday Review* vol 33 no. 870, 29 June 1872.

15   **'The yard does not vary'** A. Lloyd James, *Broadcast English*, London (British Broadcasting Corporation) 1928.

PEOPLE

20   **'Its men are mainly'** John Hollingshead, *Ragged London in 1861*, London 1861.

22   The quotes related to art appreciation are from The *Daily Telegraph*, 26 June 1872; The *Echo*, 6 July 1872 and *Atlantic Monthly,* January 1873, the latter by Henry James.

23   The 1950s quotes about liking Bethnal Green are from *Family and Kinship*. The 1960s quotes are from Peter Willmott, *Adolescent Boys of East London*, revised edition 1969.

SLANDER

24   *The Bethnal Green Slander* by William Milton exists as a broadsheet published by E. Ryner, Commercial Road, 1872. There is a copy in Tower Hamlets Local History Library.

24-7 This account of the slander is based on: The *Daily News*, 25 June 1872; *The Times*, 25 June 1872; The *Daily Telegraph*, 25 and 26 June 1872; The *Echo*, 6 July 1872; also see a letter from Septimus Hansard, *The Times*, 29 June 1872.

CHAPTER 2 pp. 29–45

29   The Henry James quote is from *Atlantic Monthly*, January 1873. The Walter Besant quote is from a speech given in Manchester and Birmingham 1884-5, reprinted in *As we are and As we may be*, London 1903.

EDUCATION

30-3 This account of the establishment of the museum is based on correspondence between the Treasury and the Science and Art Department 1866–1872 held in the National Archives, ED84/244. The quotes are all from this source. Some of the key phrases also appear in the London County Council's printed memorandum on the history of the museum, LCC/ TEB 80 (held in London Metropolitan Archives). The Henry Cole quote on page 32 is from *Fifty Years of the Public Works of Sir Henry Cole*, 1884, volume 1. For further background about the Science and Art Department's museum activities see Anthony Burton *Vision and Accident: the story of the Victoria and Albert Museum*, London 1999; and A.S. Bishop, *The Rise of a Central Authority for English Education*, Cambridge 1971.

33-5 The quotes related to the reception of the museum come from the *Saturday Review*, volume 33, number 870, 29 June 1872; and *The Metropolitan*, 4 May 1872. The quotes about the collection come from *A brief guide to the Bethnal Green branch of the South Kensington Museum*, London 1872, and a separate brief guide to the Food Collection.

38   **'I may be wrong'** ED 84/233, particularly a memorandum of 25 July 1873, investigating transfer of South Kensington's entire empire, including Bethnal Green, to the British Museum's trustees. Also see ED 84/30 for more on this Treasury attempt to curb South Kensington.

39   The Cecil Smith quote is from a memorandum, 29 April 1914 in ED24/601, responding to a proposal from Herbert Llewellyn Smith to start a new museum of industrial art.

40   **'To be wholeheartedly displayed'** Fiona McCarthy in The *Guardian* 11 November 1966.

40   **'Urgent disposal'** Report of the sub-committee on the Bethnal Green Museum, 20 November 1922 in ED84/115

PROPERTY

41   The Sunday opening episode is discussed in *Hansard* 11 July 1872. The question of Sunday opening at Bethnal Green remained touchy: see *The Times*, 26 May and 12 June 1873.

42   The *Illustrated London News* quote is from 29 June 1872.

42   For Lane Fox see *Journal of the Anthropological Institute*, 1875 volume 4, 'Report of a special meeting at

the Bethnal Green Museum on the occasion of the opening of the collection to the public'; and *Journal Of the Society of Arts*, vol.XL,18 December 1891.

42 **'five small darts'** ED 84/24, out letters of the Bethnal Green Museum, 1873-8. Letter of 4 September 1874.

43 **'The householders'** *The Times*, 25 June 1872.

43 **'The visitors round about us'**, A.R. Buckland, 'Bank Holiday at Bethnal Green', *Cassell's Family Magazine*, 1883.

CHAPTER 3 pp. 47–69

47 Charles Greville's diary for 17 February 1832 is reproduced in *Memoirs* volume 1, London 1874.

47 **'by mid-century silk weaving'** David R Green, *From Artisans to Paupers*, Aldershot, 1995 which contains much further detail about the crisis in poor law administration which produced such hardship in Bethnal Green.

48 **'I'm sure if the ladies'** Henry Mayhew, 'And ye shall walk in silk attire', written in the 1840s but published in *London Characters,* London 1881.

SILK

49–52 This account of the industry is based on: Frank Warner, *History of the Silk Industry*, London 1921: Alfred Plummer, *The London Weavers Company*, 1600–1970, 1972 and H. L. Smith, *A History of East London*, London 1939; G.R. Porter, Treatise on the Silk Manufacture, London 1831. The Henry Parnell quote on page 51 is from *On Financial Reform*, London 1831 and refers to glovemaking as well as silk weaving.

52 The quotes about the clannishness and feebleness of the weavers are from The Report of the Assistant Commissioners on Hand-Loom Weavers, pt. II, February 1840. The Francis Place quote is from his evidence to the 1835 committee on education, quoted in Dorothy George, *London life in the 18th century* which also contains further detail about the weavers in this period. The letter from the Rev. James Trevitt was printed in *The Times*, 17 February 1853.

FILTH

53–6 This section is based on various journalistic accounts of conditions in Bethnal Green and Spitalfields. See in particular *The Times*, 13 November 1841 'Distress in Spitalfields'; *The Times*, 8 October 1842; *The Builder*, 28 May and 4 June 1853; The *Illustrated London News*, 24 October 1863 'Dwellings of the poor in Bethnal Green'; *The Builder*, 28 January 1871.'Homes in the east of London, a fresh visit to Bethnal Green'.

53 Alexis Soyer's letters to the Times in the 1840s are all reprinted in *Memoirs of Alexis Soyer*, ed. F. Volant and J.R. Warren, London 1859.

56 The end of apprenticeships in Bethnal Green is mentioned in *Report to the Secretary of State for the Home Department from the Poor Law Commission on the Training of Pauper Children*, London 1841.

CRAFTSMANSHIP

58–9 Admiring descriptions of the surviving elderly weavers are found in: 'A Vanishing Industry', The *Daily Graphic*, 7 April 1899; The weavers of Spitalfields', *The Lady*, 21 May 1914; *The Londoner*, July 1934; *The Daily Chronicle*, 3 March 1928 (reprinted in A.K. Sabin, *The Silkweavers of Spitalfields and Bethnal Green*, 1931); *Industrial World*, August 1929 (also reprinted in Sabin, 1931); and H.V. Morton 'Last of the Huguenot weavers' in *Ghosts of London*, 1926. Bishop Paget's quote is from his chapter on 'The East End' in *London of the Future*, ed. A Webb, London 1921

63 Hubert Llewellyn Smith's Report to the Special Committee on Technical Education, 1892 is found in the LCC papers at London Metropolitan Archives, LCC/ TEB 79a.

64 **'This is shown'** Luther Hooper, *Hand-loom Weaving, plain and ornamental*, London 1910.

64 The account of Morris's interest in weaving, is based on Linda Parry, *William Morris Textiles*, London 1983, which also includes the quote reproduced here.

CROWN

67 **'The young weaver'** *Eastern Argus*, 18 July 1893.

67 The 1830 meeting is reported in the *Standard*, 1 November 1830.

69 The quotes about the demolition of the weavers cottages are from the *The Times*, 13 January 1958 and *Architect and Building News*, 22 January 1958, both in Tower Hamlets Local History Library, which also holds good photographs of the demolished cottages.

CHAPTER 4 pp. 71–95

72 The George Orwell quotes are all from, *The English People*, London 1947. Young and Willmott's explanation of their aims is from Michael Young and Peter Willmott. 'Research Report no.3, the Institute of Community Studies at Bethnal Green', *Sociological Review*, July 1961.

VILLAGE

72–7 Glass and Frankel are the main sources for this section, but also see J.H. Forshaw and Patrick Abercrombie, *County of London Plan*, 1943 and Ronald Frankenberg, *Communities in Britain: social life in town and country*, London 1966, for another version of Glass and Frankel's portrait of Bethnal Green as an egalitarian village. For the older 'stagnant' theory, see Robert Sinclair, *East London*, London 1956 and its source: Hubert Llewellyn Smith, 'Influx of Population (East London)', chapter 2 in Charles Booth, *Life and Labour of the People in London*, 1st series, volume III.

HOUSING

78 The Colin Ward quote is from 'Bethnal Green a museum of housing', talk broadcast on the BBC Third Programme, 6 December 1962, reprinted in *Housing, an Anarchist Approach*, London 1973, and in turn included in notes by Elaine Harwood 'Bethnal Green a Museum of Housing' accompanying a 20th Century Society walk, 1992. The latter also adds further detail about post-war housing in Bethnal Green.

80–1 The quotes in this section are from *Family and Kinship* plus Young and Willmott's later publication: Michael Young and Peter Willmott, *Family and Class in a London Suburb*, London 1960.

82 **'a combination of'** D.C. Bailey 'New Architecture', in *East London Papers*, volume 4 no.1, April 1961.

82–4 Michael Young's 1980 reflection on tower blocks is from Michael Young et al. *Report from Hackney, a study of an inner city area*, London 1980. The interview with Michael Young is from the *Sunday Times*, 3 June 2001.

85 The gist of the Smithson's 1953 presentation to CIAM is reproduced in Theo Crosby, *Urban Structuring*, London 1967.

OUTSIDERS

85–9 The main source for this section is James Robb, *Working-class Anti-Semite: a psychological study in a London borough*, London 1954. Other quotes are from Young and Wilmott, and PJO Self. The quotes related to the Jewish population are from Constance Harris, Llewellyn Smith and Bishop Paget's chapter on 'The East End' in *London of the Future*, ed. A Webb, London 1921.

ART

92–5 The inital quote is from Nigel Henderson, *Photographs of Bethnal Green, 1949–52*, Nottingham 1978. This is the main source for this section, along with *Nigel Henderson, paintings, collages and photographs*, catalogue of an exhibition at Anthony d'Offay, September–October 1977; Judith Henderson's manuscript diary December 1946–June 1947 in Tate Archive, Nigel Henderson papers List K9; and James Lingwood's essay on Henderson in *The Independent Group: postwar Britain and the Aesthetics of Plenty*, ed. David Robbins, Cambridge Mass, 1990. This extremely useful catalogue also reproduces contemporary critical writing about the Independent Group's artists and activities. The quotes related to This is Tomorrow and the Smithsons' account of the 'as found aesthetic' are all taken from here and Theo Crosby, *Urban Structuring*, London 1967.

CHAPTER 5 pp. 97–113

97–8 The letters from Edward Ponsonby quoted here are from the, *East London Advertiser*, 4 February and 1 March 2005; also see letter from Norman Sampson, 4 March 2005, and from John Rush, 11 March 2005.

DEATH

100 The anecdote about Oxford House residents and swearing is quoted in Mandy Ashworth, *The Oxford House in Bethnal Green*, London 1984.

101 The 'English rose' quote is from a letter by G. Cope, printed in the *East London Advertiser*, 2 September, 2004. For cockney orientalism see H.V. Morton, 'A bit of Baghdad in the Heart of London', 1925, reprinted in *H.V. Morton's London*, 1940.

102 For the Kray funerals see the *Independent*, 20 April 2000; William Leith, 'Gangster Chic' in the *Evening Standard*, 20 April 2000; letter from Joyce Gordon, the *Independent*, 3 October 2000; letter from Robert Kavanagh, the *Evening Standard*, 25 April 2000.

LIFE

105 **'Stepney is the coloured man's district'** Michael Barton, *The Coloured Quarter*, London 1953.

106 The 1995 survey of residents is discussed in Mike Fenton 'Living in Bethnal Green: together or apart' in *London: the Promised Land?,* ed. Anne Kershen, London 1997.

107 The 'Me and My Home' property feature was in the *Independent*, 9 February 2005.

107 The Harry King quote is from an interview with Sally Musgrave, 4 September 1998 transcribed on vads.ahds.ac.uk/collections/oep/harryking/ which contains further details about the group of artists established during the 1970s around Approach Road and the Acme studios in Robinson Road.

ROMANCE

113 Beryl Horne's poem appeared on the letters page of the *East London Advertiser* in January 1997.